Violent Voices:

12 Steps To Freedom From Verbal And Emotional Abuse

Kay Marie Porterfield

Health Communications, Inc.
Deerfield Beach, Florida

Kay Marie Porterfield
Denver, Colorado

Library of Congress Cataloging-in-Publication Data

Porterfield, Kay Marie.
    Violent Voices: 12 steps to freedom from emotional abuse/
by Kay Marie Porterfield.
        p.   cm.
    ISBN 1-55874-028-7
    1. Abused women — Psychology.   2. Relationship addic-
tion.   3. Self-help techniques.   I. Title.
HV1444.P67   1989   89-1979
362.8'3—dc19   CIP

© 1989 Kay Marie Porterfield
ISBN 1-55874-028-7

Published by: Health Communications, Inc.
              3201 S.W. 15th Street
              Deerfield Beach, Florida 33442

Cover Design by Reta Thomas

Contents

To D.J.M. who is
wise beyond his years.

Introduction

Women enmeshed with verbally and emotionally abusive partners suffer deep wounds. Because our injuries aren't readily visible to the eye, we endure our private agony in silence. Mistrusting our perceptions, we often deny to ourselves and to others the existence of our very real pain.

This is changing as psychologists and domestic violence specialists recognize verbal and emotional abuse as a problem with severe psychological and physical consequences for those of us who serve as targets. With the publication of Robin Norwood's bestselling book, *Women Who Love Too Much*, and Dr. Susan Forward's book, *Men Who Hate Women and the Women Who Love Them*, our silent shame is a secret no longer. We know without a doubt that we are not alone. Millions of women came forward to buy these books, enough women to put Norwood's book on *The New York Times* Bestseller List.

Today in every major city self-help groups exist for those of us struggling to regain our self-esteem and extricate ourselves from emotionally poisonous relationships with men, relationships every bit as dangerously addictive as alcohol or drugs. Finally we have validation for our feelings, help in coping with them and hope for recovery.

Out of our intense emotional pain springs the desire to change. Because we have *learned* to serve as psychic targets for the negative feelings of others, we can now begin to learn how not to be psychological scapegoats, can learn to be the strong, capable and loving women we were born to be. Out of our distress we learn to mend first ourselves, then our relationships with others and with the Sacred.

Our healing process takes place on at least three levels. Obviously verbal and emotional violence cause psychological wounds. In the midst of a one-down relationship our thoughts swirl in negative spirals, and our feelings chaotically writhe and twist so it's often impossible for us to make sense out of them, let alone give name to them.

Just as obviously, our external reality, including our relationship to other people, is deformed into a grim parody of meaningful rewarding interaction.

Not so obviously, emotional abuse leaves severe spiritual scars as well. When we disconnect from ourselves, we in turn sever our relationship with the Divine. We no longer sense the caring presence of our Higher Power and forget that we are part of a much larger scheme of things than is apparent from our day to day existence. As John Bradshaw, a nationally noted expert on dysfunctional families, so aptly puts it — we have a hole in our soul.

The Twelve Steps of Alcoholics Anonymous speak directly to the three kinds of healing that we so desperately need. They help us reclaim ourselves and reconnect with others and our Higher Power one step at a time. The Steps gently guide us from the hurting through the healing to emotional, relational and spiritual health. In time we fill in the holes in our souls and become truly whole, some of us for the first time in our lives. For women who were emotionally, physically or sexually abused as children, the process isn't one of recovery — how can we take back something we never can recall having? It's a process of discovery, finding out for the first time who we are and where we want to be.

Because the Twelve Steps are so effective, and because they are a powerful method of healing our emotional, interpersonal and spiritual wounds, this book is based upon them. It can be both a guide and a source of support as you direct your energies to the self-healing process.

The important thing to remember is that there is no universal timetable for recuperating from verbal or emotional violence. Your healing journey will happen at your own rate.

Some days you'll be amazed and overjoyed with your progress, and at other times you'll feel stuck. Just because you don't happen to be aware of the healing that is occurring at any given moment, doesn't mean that it isn't happening. Important changes transpire beneath your level of consciousness as long as you continue to read and work the Steps. Our conscious minds sometimes have a difficult time adjusting to change, and that's just what healing is — a transformation. Even when our conscious thought process takes a breather, at a deeper level we're still getting better.

As you practice the Steps, you may find yourself struggling and, in your impatience, psychologically abusing yourself for not being smart enough or fast enough or strong enough. When this happens, be aware that you've absorbed the negative messages you've heard about yourself in the past and accepted them as the truth about who you are, no matter how wrong those messages were. Recognize this negative habit when it rears its head, then let the feeling go and replace the denial of your self-worth with its opposite affirmation.

I am as intelligent and strong as I need to be at this moment, and I'm starting to heal at a pace that is right for me.

1

❧

Is Your Relationship Hazardous
To Your Mental Health?

"Self-love depressed becomes self-loathing."

Sally Kempton
Cutting Loose

Before we can begin our healing journey, we need to become familiar with the problem that plagues us. Verbal violence, mental cruelty, emotional abuse are difficult terms to define. Every woman, no matter what her upbringing was or who her partner is, sometimes feels put upon. Rarely do real-live relationships match romantic fantasies. Given the added stress of living in a culture where male and female roles are in a state of flux, we may at times feel confused and angry at our partners for not living up to our expectations.

Once in a while all women will question whether the men in their lives really love them, wish they were more sensitive and crave more attention from them. Men on occasion have the same feelings about their wives and

1

girlfriends. Marital conflicts aren't always resolved with win/win solutions. Sometimes he wins and sometimes she does. Such struggles and temporary imbalances are a normal part of caring long-term relationships.

The life of a woman involved in a verbally and psychologically abusive relationship is a different story. It is filled with arguments she invariably loses, losing her sense of self in the process. The jarring assaults on her self-esteem, whether weekly or daily, leave her psyche dented and scarred. Abuse, no matter whether the weapons are words, mind games or fists, is akin to brainwashing.

Fearful of what dehumanizing threat or insult lurks around the next corner, those of us subjected to such mental torments may start out agreeing with our abusive partner's definitions of reality and of ourselves only to keep peace and protect ourselves. Before long, however, our inner core weakens, and we accept his perceptions and values as the only correct ones, his needs and wishes as the only valid ones. When he is not present, we find ourselves using his words to castigate ourselves. Even though we may get together the courage to leave an emotionally abusive relationship, some of us become enmeshed in yet another one almost immediately. We've become our own worst enemies.

In their book, *Battering Men,* authors Daniel Jay Sonkin, Del Martin and Lenore Walker define psychological violence as "ways of controlling, dominating and intimidating another person." Such bullying methods, over time, generate fear and compliance from their targets. On one level they work; the abuser gets his point across and gets his way. But on a deeper level he fails because he senses his victim is bound to him by fear. Although she may love him, her survival instinct, not love, motivates her compliance. His insecurity and anger mount, and he again discharges it, often blowing up in disproportion to the event which triggered the outburst.

The most minor annoyances become a big deal to the verbally abusive rage-aholic. The feelings of control and power he experiences from using intimidating behavior grow less and less satisfying. When he needs another outrage fix, he'll focus on anything handy, even if it's yelling at you for doing something he explicitly ordered you to do the day before. No matter how hard you try, pleasing him is an impossible task.

You are a scapegoat, accepting the burden of his anger demons, feeling the hurt he refuses to face. In time the abusive exchanges take on an almost ritualistic character. Even though you may never know when to expect the next outburst, his insults and put-downs are a liturgy of rage and pain that you know by heart. Through control and manipulation he tries to sacrifice your self-esteem in order to save his own. Like the scapegoating rituals of ancient times, his must be repeated over and over again because it never quite works.

Anatomy Of An Emotional Abuser

It's important to understand that not all men who are verbal and psychological abusers handle their anger inappropriately in every situation. The man who would never threaten to bash his boss's brains in with a heavy glass ashtray feels perfectly at ease verbalizing that threat to his wife if she comes home five minutes late. His co-workers may regard him as the soul of gentleness, but at home he acts like a different person.

Even though he operates under the assumption that he can't help himself and that we force him into his fits of temper, he (not we) has volition over how he communicates his anger. Frequently he discharges his rage only in the relative safety of his home and only when he views his target as smaller and weaker than himself. Beneath the bully exterior lurks an emotional coward who is just as likely to have a college education, a good job and church membership as not.

Neither is his reign of terror in full operation every minute of every day. There are times when he's a delight to be around, times when he's thoughtful and loving.

There are good days and even weeks in our relationships with emotional abusers as well as bad ones, so we hold onto the hope that the harmony will last. Unfortunately, it doesn't. We walk on eggs, trying desperately not to upset the delicate balance until inadvertently we spend an hour talking on the phone with a friend instead of watching him watch TV or we try a new recipe for dinner and it doesn't work out.

"You don't love me," he storms. "You're out to get me!" And he's off on another tirade, lecturing us that his foul mood is all our fault.

The unpredictability of his actions, combined with his periods of good behavior, conspire to form an especially intense bond between him and his victim. We cling to the false hope during the good times that he's really changing. We excuse and explain away his outbursts and manipulations. During the bad times, we allow ourselves to be convinced that without him we are nothing.

When animals are given shocks only sporadically as they reach for food pellets, they begin to show severe stress reactions since they can never predict what will happen next. They begin compulsively reaching for food and it is very difficult to teach them to stop. Intermittent reinforcement is a much more powerful teacher than no reinforcement at all.

It's that way with human beings, too. If when we seek affection, we are sometimes hugged and sometimes called demanding bitches, we reach out to our mates all the more frantically. When the times he's nicest to us occur right after the abuse in an attempt to make up, we may come to regard mistreatment as the price we must pay for affection and positive attention.

Varieties Of Emotional Abuse

Emotional abuse comes in many varieties. Some men rely primarily on words in order to intimidate their partners. Other invade their spouse's privacy or play on her fears. One man's methods of subjugation aren't necessarily the same another might use. According to Sonkin, Martin and Walker, there are several common subcategories of psychologically abusive behavior.

Threats Of Violence

The most clearly recognizable abusive manipulation is an explicit threat of violence.

"I feel like wringing your neck, just to shut you up," Arnold would yell at his wife, Cynthia, whenever she disagreed with him or requested that he do housework. "If you don't stop that, I'll break your arm," and, "How'd you like a fat lip?" are other examples of this control strategy. Although Arnold has never hit Cynthia, she knew that if he did carry out his threats, he could do a great deal of physical damage to her. His fist pounding and loud voice led her to believe that his anger was out of control. As long as there was a chance he might make good on his threats, she didn't want to take the risk of becoming his punching bag.

Explicit threats are far more potent to women who have been beaten by their partners. Even if the physical abuse happened once long ago, and it hasn't recurred, we still carry the mental and emotional scars inside of us. We know for a fact the man in question is capable of breaking our bones and blacking our eyes, and we want to avoid a repeat performance at all costs.

Implied Threats

The second category of psychological abuse involves implicit threats of violence.

Jerry had beaten Linda severely twice during the early years of their marriage. He had raped her once. At the time both were drinking. When the addictive drinking stopped, so did the violence but not the threat that it could happen again. Whenever the couple got into an argument, Jerry leapt up and paced back and forth like a furious tiger, his hands curled into fists which he brandished as he made his points. Although he never said outright that he was going to hit her if she didn't back down and let him win the argument, he didn't have to.

"If you do that one more time, I'm not responsible for what I do," he'd hint broadly, his neck muscles knotted and his face red. Invariably Linda would apologize, and tranquility was restored in their relationship until the next time conflict arose.

When we're faced with implied threats, we can never be quite sure where real intentions leave off and our imagination begins. To protect ourselves, we attempt to de-escalate the angry situation. Later when we confront him with his behavior, we're told our perceptions were all wrong. "I never said I was going to hit you," he says with a look of hurt on his face. "How could you ever believe I'd do such a thing?" In truth our belief comes from picking up very real signals of impending danger. Clenched fists are the same as a dog's growl and bared teeth. They provoke an immediate surge of adrenaline and a visceral response of fear. When we cannot flee, we learn to submit.

Violence Against Property

Destruction of property also sends a clear message to a woman that if she isn't careful, she may be the next to be punched out after the wall. Violence such as throwing dishes, chairs and record albums, ripping or slashing clothing and kicking down doors serves to intimidate onlookers into submission.

"I got carried away," was Tom's response the morning after he knocked over a bookcase and ripped up three hundred dollars worth of his live-in lover's college textbooks. Then he shrugged and gave her his little boy grin. She was so relieved, she made him a special breakfast and dropped the subject.

When a small child has a temper tantrum, we can afford to ignore him or carry him to his room where he can wind down. When a grown man has a similar tantrum, we're physically outclassed and we, as well as he, know it. Under such circumstances, we often feel terrified for our own safety and give in to our mate's demands, even though we know deep inside we're giving up our integrity and our dignity. The destruction of belongings that are important to us is his powerful and symbolic way to teach us that he is boss and if we protest, we'll be punished.

Controlling

Extreme controlling behavior is another technique some men use to gain a dominant position over the women they live with.

It was Nathan who dictated when his wife and children would eat, what they would eat, as well as the temperature of the house, what reading material would come into the home and what everyone would wear. If an outing was planned, he would stall, making other members of his family wait for him for hours. If they were the cause of a five-minute delay, he would pout and cancel the excursion. No matter whether the decision at hand was what kind of car or what kind of toothpaste to use, Nathan insisted on having the final say.

"He acts like a little boy," Pam, his wife, would tell herself, but over time his behavior ceased to be amusing. He insisted that she watch TV with him during the evening and that the lights be out. This prevented her from grading the papers she often needed to take home from her teaching job. If she worked in the other room where she could see, he stopped speaking to her for hours. If she asked him to turn on a light, he refused. In all areas of their relationship things had to be done Nathan's way or not at all.

Other emotionally abusive men control by dictating whom their wives will and will not see and how they will spend the money they, themselves, earn. Some control in bed by withholding foreplay or routinely stopping it to deny their lovers pleasure. Others withhold sex or demand that it take place whenever they want.

A few insist on driving their wives to work or school and picking them up under the guise of helpfulness when in reality, they're making sure these women don't go out of the house unsupervised.

Whether blatantly or covertly, the controller demands to be dictator, ruling the woman he claims to love. Once she becomes accustomed to having no power over even the smallest details of her life, she may actually become helpless and incompetent, resentful of his control over her, yet terrified that she cannot survive without him. She comes to view herself as a child and he, the authoritarian parent, who tells her what to do and punishes her if she disobeys.

Isolation

This is one of the most potent forms of control a man can use against his mate. At dismal best he discourages friendships with other people by sulking and withdrawing, at worst he forbids them, threatening to leave her or to physically abuse her if she doesn't meet his need to be the center of her life at all times. In time she may come to believe she is not worthy of friendship. She becomes a psychological prisoner in solitary confinement, her will broken.

Sarah had heard so many times from her husband, James, that she was neurotic, she was terrified to have social conversations with the people she worked with out of fear they'd see her "craziness" and reject her. At the start of their relationship they had some social contact with friends, but that ended when James began criticizing her after evenings out.

"You embarrassed me," he'd lecture. "Every time you open your mouth, something dumb comes out. You're socially inept and you make my friends uncomfortable. I'm ashamed to be seen with you!" By the time he told her to quit her job, she readily agreed, certain she would eventually lose it when her employers discovered the personality defects James continually pointed out "for her own good." Afterward she spent her days alone and soon sank into depression.

When a woman allows her mate to isolate her through threats or intimidation, she cuts off valuable support systems. No on can meet her needs except for him and that gives him an immense amount of power over her emotional state. When he withdraws or withholds love, there is no one else to love her, and she feels crushed. Because she doesn't have contact with other people, she loses perspective about how other people relate to her and her worth as a human being. It becomes second nature to automatically accept his views on marriage as the only ones available, his opinion of her as infallible. As her loneliness increases, so does her dependency on him and her fears that she is incapable and undeserving of friendship.

Extreme Jealousy

Accusations of unfaithfulness are yet another psychologically crushing method of abuse. While most spouses feel jealous at times, the emotional abuser's low opinion of his competence as a mate keeps him constantly on guard against *his* woman abandoning him. He may insist that she account for each minute she's away from him, grill her about phone calls and letters and make irrational charges.

Katherine's husband, Peter, accused her of having an affair whenever she disagreed with him. She found herself constantly defending her loyalty to him to no avail. He opened her mail and read it carefully looking for clues. When she went on a diet, he was convinced she had a lover. If he called her from work and she was at the grocery store, she had to produce a receipt as evidence of her whereabouts when he returned home at night. Evenings when she wasn't in the mood for sex, he raged that she was spending her afternoons in bed with another man. Many times he called her a slut and a whore and although she struggled to feel good about her own sexuality, she began to believe that she was somehow dirty and bad. Eventually her entire life focused around reassuring him and bolstering his fragile ego.

Ironically, the intense jealousy men like Peter display has the opposite effect from the one they intend. When we're accused of things we haven't done and thoughts we haven't thought, we grow resentful. Although we may dedicate ourselves to reassuring our spouse that he's the only man we want, need and love, inside we pull away from him. Often under these circumstances, sex becomes a duty for us and we become distant in the bedroom, present in body but not in spirit. When an extremely jealous husband senses this, his discomfort adds more fuel to the rage.

Mental Cruelty

One of the most common emotionally manipulative techniques abusive men use against their wives and lovers is mental degradation, name-calling and put-downs. "You never do anything right," "You're a frigid, asexual bitch," and "It's all your fault," chip away at our self-esteem if we hear them often enough, especially from someone who knows us well and who claims to love us.

These verbal mind games are usually aimed at the spots where we're least secure. If we aren't comfortable with the way we look, he's right there to criticize our thighs. Often he does this in a back-handed manner. "Some men might think you have fat legs," he tells you, "but your cellulite doesn't bother me." When you express hurt, he becomes infuriated. You've misinterpreted him. You're too sensitive. You're putting words in his mouth. How dare you even think he'd be so manipulative and mean?

Nancy, who'd grown up with a cold and emotionally inaccessible father, feared abandonment. Kyle, her husband, repeatedly reported how several women at work were after him and how tempting it was for him to have an affair whenever they had a disagreement or a sexual slump. When she asked if he was making a threat, he demurred. He was just stating the facts, important facts she should know about. He used this tactic repeatedly to set off cycles of selfish sex which were gratifying to him, but left Nancy tense and frustrated. She managed to play the game by convincing herself she didn't deserve to feel good, but she paid a price for her compliance, suffering from intense muscle spasms so painful, she was in tears much of the time.

The put-down artist may criticize his partner for being too dumb or too smart, too passive or too assertive, sometimes leveling both charges in the same argument. He makes fun of her beliefs, her tastes and her mannerisms. Nothing is spared his disapproval, even her "sins" from the distant past or things she can't control like her height or her monthly period.

The words he uses during his rages are highly charged and often replete with psychological meaning. His partner is paranoid; she's acting schizophrenic; she's crazy. He uses hyperbole. "She *always* says the wrong thing. She *never* does anything right." He compares her to other women he's known and she comes up short.

Heard day after day, week after week, these insults etch their way into our thinking until they become our reality. We put ourselves down with his phrases even when he's not around. His domination is so complete, we emotionally batter ourselves and save him the effort except for occasional reinforcing outbursts. We deny our worth as human beings.

The opposite of denial is affirmation. When those we love do not affirm our value as human beings, we need to be able to affirm ourselves. Until we can do this we are as much victims of our own low self image as we are of his anger.

> *I am a competent and lovable human being. When others reject me, I still value and love myself.*

2

✦

The Insidious Nature Of Verbal Abuse: Why We Tolerate It

"If we would have new knowledge, we must get a whole world of new questions."

Susan Langer
Philosophy In A New Key

Sticks and stones may break our bones, we were told as children, but words can never hurt us. They can. They do. Sharp tongues wound. Language is the symbolic representation of our innermost feelings and beliefs, and potent words call up a host of vivid associations, either positive or negative. Angry, damning words heard over and over again tend to be believed. When we deny the process and potency of put downs, condemnations and sharp criticisms, we are unable to counter the negative spell they cast over us. Even though we live in the Twentieth Century, none of us is immune from the almost magical power of words. They can hurt us. They can help to heal us.

13

Because verbal abuse leaves no physical marks except for stress-related symptoms (which we can readily blame on other causes), it has been easy for mental health professionals, law enforcement officials and women victims, themselves, to avoid calling verbal and emotional abuse into question. Emotionally abused women have tended to fall through the cracks — even those of us who develop drinking problems, prescription drug addictions, compulsive-eating disorders or stress-related illnesses, like high blood pressure and chronic headaches. Once we acknowledge that psychological victimization isn't our due, we begin to wonder why we as individuals and as society have tolerated it for so long.

Since psychologically and verbally abusing men often function very well in their other roles, confining their flagrantly manipulative tempers to their homes, we are often the only witnesses to maltreatment. We're often afraid to share our stories out of fear of being laughed at or told by someone other than the man who has become our judge and jury that we deserve his rage and cruelty, that all we need to do is to be good wives and everything will be fine. Our fear of further rejection freezes us into inaction.

Many emotional abusers act out their rage in only one or two arenas of the relationship — they aren't totally misogynistic. He may insist that you turn your paycheck over to him, then give you an allowance which is inadequate for the household expenses and yell in fury for hours when you exceed the impossible budget, but at least he doesn't threaten to hit you or threaten to leave. Or maybe, like Peter, he's extremely jealous and constantly tells you that you dress and act like a whore, but at least he's a good provider and he remembers your birthday. Perhaps he constantly criticizes you for being such a castrating bitch if you dare to disagree with one of his opinions, but at least he's great in bed.

Often we focus on his good points and try to turn a blind eye to the oppressive reality of his temper. Even if he doesn't abuse alcohol or drugs, even if he doesn't beat us, those positives don't cancel out the negative effects of verbal and psychological abuse on our physical, emotional and spiritual lives. The abuse is real. Our pain is real.

We live in a society that rewards men for being aggressive and women for being passive. Anyone who thinks the macho image is a thing of the past need only sit through *Rambo* or take a look at the box office draw for the movie to know that rigid sexual roles are still a part of our culture. We have become desensitized to abusive behavior when it's directed at women. In an environment where women validate themselves with relationships with men, and men are validated by grabbing power and being in control, it is no wonder we turn our heads away from the psychological violence we see inflicted on other women and that our spouses and lovers inflict upon us. For some of us, to admit that we have a negative relationship is the same as admitting we aren't feminine.

Some women move a step further, telling themselves they don't like or deserve the way he's behaving, but *all* men are like that — aren't they? When they read women's magazines or even feminist books, they train themselves to skim over the parts that tell about men's gentleness, nurturing abilities, sensitivity, kindness and empathy. Instead they look for evidence that the man they live with is typical in the way he treats them.

For instance, when such a woman reads about male versus female speech habits, how men tend to control conversations by interrupting and switching subjects, she stretches the point to include his threats to kick the cat to death if she doesn't shut up about needing money to fix the washing machine.

Selective Perception

We develop selective perception, only absorbing information which confirms that we have a perfectly healthy relationship, filtering out perceptions that would lead us to view our situation as it really is or to feel our pain specifically and individually.

At the same time we tell ourselves that men and women should be equals, we shrug our shoulders and generalize that in the real world women will always be subservient. When we label verbal and emotional abuse as the battle between the sexes, a universal problem instead of our own, we distance ourselves from what is happening to us. We also slide out from under the responsibility of taking steps to better our lives. When you're up against a centuries-old problem, what can you do but tolerate it?

Some people (and more than a few emotional abusers among them) go so far as to use the overwhelming popularity of books like *Women Who Love Too Much* to discount the seriousness of emotional abuse. Since so many women buy these books, they rationalize, the behaviors the authors describe can't be abusive — they must be normal, so are harmless. Facts point to the contrary. In a study of 2,143 American families, researchers Murray Straus, Richard Gelles and Suzanne Steinmetz found that most of the couples for whom verbal aggression was a way of life had physically abusive marriages as well. Over 80% of the extremely verbally aggressive relationships were also physically violent. In contrast, less than half of one percent of the seldom verbally aggressive couples ever came to blows.

Cycles Of Abuse

Not only is there correlation between verbal and physical violence, but the behavior patterns of physically abusive men and those of their verbally and emotionally abusive counterparts is remarkably similar.

Abuse of any kind tends to be cyclical. For a period of time the pressure builds like the electrical charge in thunder clouds. He blows his top in a lightning flash of discharged rage. Afterwards the sun comes out. He may apologize for his unacceptable behavior but more than likely he denies it or blames his wife. Nonetheless, he is on his good behavior for a while, telling her how much he loves her, showing physical affection and perhaps even buying presents. All the time, his rage is massing again into sullen storm clouds and soon something happens to set him off again. When the tension build-up becomes untenable for her, she may consciously or subconsciously trigger an attack to get it over with. The severity of the physical, emotional and verbal batterings tends to escalate over time. Once a boundary has been crossed, it is almost impossible to retreat to a nonviolent method of handling conflict without treatment. Even though a psychological abuse victim may not have a bloody nose or a broken wrist, the psychological damage she sustains can be overwhelming.

The Catharsis Theory

Some of us have sought help from professional mental health workers subscribing to the let-it-all-hang-out catharsis theories of anger popularized in the past decade. Despite convincing evidence that verbal outbursts intensify anger rather than release it, professional helpers who adhere to the catharsis school of anger may label a verbally abusive husband's rages as positive and healthy expressions of his feelings. They encourage angry men to let a partner have it with words, to punch pillows and to bash their spouses with foam bats.

While such heated verbal and limited physical battles may work when both husband and wife are equally matched, if one or the other is frequently in the underdog position, the tirades are simply a repetition of what goes on at home. They can serve as rehearsals for more abusive behavior and rationalizations for the next verbal assault. When a therapist who is well meaning, but untrained in the signs of chronic domestic abuse, labels verbal attack as a healthy way of relating, he gives the already despotic husband permission to escalate while judging the wife as resistant to treatment for protesting. She's the one with the problem; something her spouse has been saying all along.

Misreading The Bible

Women who reach out to priests, rabbis and ministers may find that they, too, give their stamp of approval to abuse. If we have strict fundamentalist/religious upbringing, we may operate under the assumption that the Su-

preme Authority Figure, God, condones emotional abuse
as well. Whenever we are upset by our mate's name-
calling, threats or temper tantrums, the Bible verses we
were taught as children pop into our heads and we immediately feel sinful and guilty. Paul said that women are
supposed to submit themselves to men. It was Eve's fault
that she and Adam were evicted from Eden. Either we
were never taught, or we have forgotten Christ's warm
and positive relationships with the women he encountered
and with his mother. Either we've never read or we've
filtered out the Biblical injunctions to men to treat their
wives with love, kindness and respect. When we remain
unaware of positive and supportive religious teachings,
our faith ceases to be a comfort and becomes a torment.

Early Lessons

Many of us who stay in long-term committed relationships with verbally and emotionally violent men were
raised in extremely rigid and traditional families. The
ways our parents related to each other is one of the most
influential factors in determining the course our adult
relationships with men will take. If we lived in unhappy
ultra-traditional families, we saw our fathers rule as dic-
tators over the family, while our mothers cringed and
picked up the pieces.

Frequently we were told, "If he didn't love you, he
wouldn't yell at you like he does or he wouldn't beat you."
Or we heard, "Men are just like that. You have to stay on
their good side."

We learned to fear men, to comply with their demands,
to baby them, humor and cajole them — not how to relate
to them with honest equality. From our mothers we were
taught never to confront a man directly, but instead to go
behind his back and soften him up. We also believed the
males in the family, including our brothers, were the people
who really counted and that we existed to serve them.

Some of the "man-handling" lessons we might have
learned in girlhood are:

- "Men are little boys."
- "They can't show affection."
- "It's a woman's responsibility to keep the relationship going."
- "Make him think it was his idea in the first place and he'll agree."
- "If you want him to do something, ask him to do the opposite."
- "Marriage is supposed to make men, not women, happy."
- "A man's home is his castle."
- "Don't disagree with him; you'll only upset him."

As we grew to womanhood, we didn't stop to question these controlling and manipulative maxims. Chances are we chose to marry a man who had many of the same qualities Dad did, even though we may have thought we were rebelling against him. After all, our fathers serve as our models of what men should be like. Growing up with an emotionally distant father, one who was irresponsible, perfectionistic, demanding or psychologically cruel, sets us up to expect and accept the same sort of treatment from men as adults. We may actually feel more comfortable with this type of man than the sensitive giving sort because we don't have the foggiest idea of how to relate to men with openness and honesty. Nice guys leave us feeling off-balance.

A great number of us grew up in more blatantly dysfunctional homes. One in six women had an alcoholic parent. There are reliable indications that 16% of women, possibly more, were incested by male relatives with fathers most frequently the perpetrators. As children we may have sensed that our mother was the one in ten whose husband used physical force or threats of force to obtain sex with her. An estimated one in every three husbands hits his wife at some point during their marriage. Some of us watched our fathers routinely batter our mothers, and others were battered ourselves. Figures from a 1975 study indicate that as many as 4,000,000 children in the U.S. have been kicked, bitten or punched by a parent, and as many as three quarters of a million have been severely beaten.

Those of us who were raised under these circumstances are the walking wounded. Usually, unless we've received professional therapy, we firmly cling to the belief that we somehow brought the abuse down on ourselves. It was our fault that our parents drank, had sexual relations with us or hurt us, our fault that we did not receive the nurturing we so desperately needed. If there hadn't been something deeply wrong with us, we wouldn't have been abused, neglected or emotionally abandoned.

When we grow up, it becomes second nature to blame ourselves for bringing on our partner's verbal and emotional battering, second nature to accept the threats and tirades as our due because we are convinced we don't deserve better and there is no alternative. Even when we sense alternatives, they are unclear, and we haven't any notion of how to attain them. We're grateful our homelife isn't worse than it is compared to how we grew up.

In addition, when we were forced to meet our parents' emotional needs at the sacrifice of our own, we accept it as natural to marry a needy person and to "take care" of them at great emotional expense. If only we'd been better kids, we told ourselves, our parents would have loved us. If only we could be better adults, we tell ourselves, our spouses would respect us. We are trapped in a cycle of rejection and despair.

Whether our childhoods took place in a rigid and emotionally abusive environment or an overtly disturbed one, we grew to accept as normal the rules of the dysfunctional household: silence, rigidity, denial and isolation. They are the very regulations that have allowed us to remain compliantly in a relationship where our self-esteem was savaged on a routine basis as adults. We stuffed our feelings, sharing them with no one. We saw life in black and white and had a difficult time tolerating ambiguity — since the man we married couldn't be all bad, we viewed him as all good and ourselves as bad. We denied the bitter truth of our relationship, being hypocritical with ourselves, our husbands and our children, as well as spinning illusions for neighbors, relatives and friends. We isolated and cut ourselves off from others lest they discover the "dirty linen" of our relationships. Verbal violence, threats, manipulation and control came to equal love to us. Even when we recognized the source of our chronic anguish, sadness and panic, we felt unable to change.

Co-addiction

Today both verbal and physical violence are coming to be viewed as compulsive behavior. With that changing perception comes new hope. Women who live with men addicted to demeaning styles of relating, are co-addicts, and co-addiction, once it's recognized, can be treated.

Convinced they can't physically or psychologically survive without their abusive mate, co-addicts deny his wrongdoing with as much vehemence as he does. They cover up for him in front of the children. They enable him to abuse them, rationalizing his rage-aholic temper tantrums or agreeing with him that they were the sole cause of the argument and his inappropriate behavior. His problem becomes the central focus of their lives as they try to covertly manipulate and control his outbursts by anticipating his needs and giving in before he blows up.

Men who verbally and psychologically abuse women are emotionally troubled. If we don't have major emotional problems at the outset of the relationship, we develop them during the course of living with an abusive male. We lock our fear and hurt inside, along with the anger and resentment that someone who says he loves us could treat us in such a dehumanizing manner. We are filled with loneliness, sadness and shame — afraid to get too close to others lest they discover what our marriage is really like and hold it against us. We're ashamed to be married to a man who psychologically assaults us and guilty because

we believe that if we could just change so that he was
happy with us, he'd stop dishing out the punishment. In
time we may develop numbness, so that nothing gets to
us — he can yell all he wants, but because we've mentally
left the scene, we feel a dull emotional ache rather than a
knifing pain.

Unacknowledged Emotional Pain

Unfelt emotional pain cries out to be acknowledged in
many ways. Our shoulders are often tense and often we
suffer from lower back pain. Orgasms may become more
and more elusive with our partners and quite frequently
we lose all desire for sex. Headaches, stomach problems
and allergies can all manifest from living under constant
stress. We become jumpy, anxious and irritable. Some
experience clumsiness and are accident prone. We suffer
from sleep disorders. We may seek to soothe our denied
pain with drugs, alcohol or food.

Sticks and stones may break our bones, but rage-filled
words can and do hurt us just as deeply for they can break
our spirit. We did not willingly choose to become co-
addicts in emotionally abusive relationships — we acted as
we did because we could see no other choices.

Once we admit that we're in an addictive relationship
with an abusive man, that *we* are hurting and need help
just as much as he does, we can detach from his pain and
work on coming to grips with our own. We can't force
him to change his ways, but we can learn to take care of
ourselves, breaking our crippling dependency on emotional
pain as a way of life by working a Twelve-Step program.

*The Twelve Steps offer me the choices I have been
seeking. I willingly open myself to the hope, help and
comfort they provide.*

3

Step One

We admitted we were powerless
over the emotional and verbal abuse and that
our lives had become unmanageable.

*"Everybody knows that if you are too careful, you
are so occupied in being careful that you are sure
to stumble over something."*

Gertrude Stein

The first step we take in any new endeavor is often the
most difficult because with that step we begin to break
old habits and form unfamiliar patterns. The new is
always unknown and can be a bit frightening. As we look
back at our emotional ups and downs, at the pain we've
endured in a psychologically abusive relationship, we may
loathe the way we've lived, but it's a well-traveled path.
With this First Step, admitting that we have no power
over the emotional batterings, we start our journey away
from hurt and toward healing.

Acknowledging our powerlessness over the emotional abuse is not the same as accepting it because we're convinced we deserve it. In fact, this step moves us away from the self-destructive belief that we brought the insults and intimidation on ourselves. We are asked to give up one of our strongest defenses against the pain we feel when we are intimidated by the men we love — the illusion that we are responsible for and, therefore, in control of our psychologically abusive partner's feelings and behavior. The false sense of control which we clutch so tightly like a security blanket is a deceptive vision and not reality. It is a dangerous defense, one that often causes us to stumble.

Controlling Our Environment

All adults develop defenses. Without at least a few of them, we'd be completely vulnerable to what was happening around us, totally open and unprotected. Learning to manipulate and control the environment is part of the human growth process. Manipulation, the art of managing or operating skillfully, can be a very positive thing. We learn early on that if we're thirsty, the best way to take care of ourselves is to go into the kitchen, get a glass and manipulate the faucet to fill the glass. Unless there is a problem with the plumbing, we have mastery over meeting our need for water.

Manipulating and controlling other people in order to get our emotional needs met, however, isn't quite so direct or simple. Unlike faucets, the people in our lives have their own needs to consider, and when those needs conflict with ours, we may not get what we want from them. If we were lucky, we learned as infants that to smile would generally bring us positive attention, so today we use that as one of our tools to control the human environment. Later we learned that when we asked for something, we had a much greater chance of having our wishes granted if we said, "Please." Throughout our lives we've been collecting a series of techniques for improving the odds of getting our needs met. Without knowing exactly what we were doing, we became skillful people managers.

As humans we're more comfortable with order than with chaos and unpredictability. The more chaotic and unpredictable our immediate environment, the more vulnerable we feel and the greater is our need to rigidly control it, changing the ambiguity to certainty. The less actual power we have in a given situation, the more we need to feel powerful and in control. Our management skills become harmful, rather than helpful, when we refuse to admit there are things in our lives we can't mold to suit our purposes, and instead trick ourselves into a false sense of security with an illusion of power.

An emotionally abusive relationship presents us with an extremely inconsistent and threatening milieu. In order to defend ourselves against our fear of what will happen next, we convince ourselves that our mates are like a complicated piece of machinery. We may not be able to work them now, but once we figure out how they tick, we'll be able to get them to run smoothly. If he's broken, we'll fix him and everything will be fine.

In fact, one of the most common metaphors used to describe heated emotional exchanges between partners feeds this illusion of control.

"You're pushing my buttons," he rages. If you buy into the notion that by pushing emotional buttons, you are the direct cause of his feelings and his behavior, then you must buy the corollary that if you stop pushing his buttons, he'll be a sweetheart. Or if you push the right buttons instead of the wrong ones, everything will be fine. He has none of the power and control over himself — you have it all. Unfortunately, this line of reasoning has a major flaw. A man is not a touch-tone phone. Even if he were, the messages you receive when you push a sequence of buttons aren't pre-recorded. Their content and intensity vary, depending on circumstances beyond your control. Thinking you could stop his rages is self-deceptive and damaging.

Abusive partners collude in creating this illusion of power. An emotional batterer gives his wife the message that she has the power to infuriate him and, in effect, ruin his day or his life. Certainly he believes this to be true and makes no secret of it. He also makes no secret of his belief that she has the power to make his day or transform his life into blissful existence — if only *she* would change. This sort of rationalization lets the abuser off the hook. As long as he can deny responsibility for his behavior, there is no need for him to take a look at himself. She's the sicko and he's Mr. Mental Health.

Our power fantasy seduces us into becoming obsessed with ignoring who we are and struggling to be who he says he wants us to be. We lose touch with our own needs and become reactors rather than actors in the drama of our marriage. Often we develop rigid rituals for getting through the day without causing him upset. Although we never seem to get it right, we keep trying because if we manage to pull it off, we'll live happily ever after — all-powerful goddesses who with the wave of a magic wand or a kiss can transform another human's negative emotions and actions into positive ones. He is the frog prince and we are the princess. Unfortunately simply kissing him isn't going to make him better.

To admit we have no control over the abuse means we have to face it for what it is, intimidation and domination that we are powerless to stop. This can be a frightening revelation. Once we turn our attention from trying to control our mates, we begin to focus on ourselves and our own pain. For some of us that intense hurt began in childhood, long before we ever met the man we're involved with.

Repeating Our Childhood

Those of us who grew up in dysfunctional families are programmed to repeat the experiences we had when we were little. Since childhood we've shouldered the blame for the ways in which those around us felt and acted.

Whether a parent drank, neglected us, insulted us, beat us or forced sexual relations on us, we were told our parent's behavior was all our fault. We may have tried a number of tactics to get our parent to pay attention to us, to stop drinking or to stop touching us inappropriately. No matter what we did, our most vigorous efforts were doomed to failure.

"I'm sorry," became our automatic response to every situation. Still we heard, "If it weren't for you, I wouldn't be doing this." Not surprisingly many of us came to believe that our very existence, the fact we were on the planet, was enough to wreak havoc on the lives of those around us and inspire them to fits of depression or angry frenzy. We came to view ourselves as little gods around whom the world revolved.

Unless we confront this magical thinking, we carry it with us into adulthood. If our spouse is unhappy or angry, we don't stop to think that his depression or rage may not be triggered by us. Perhaps he's had a hard day or even a hard life that we had nothing to do with. He may feel angry toward us at times, but we do not *make* him yell insults, threaten to kill us or break every dish in the house. We are *not* the center of his universe, nor should we strive to be. When we attempt to gain that powerful position, ironically we put him in the center of *our* lives and allow ourselves to be completely at the mercy of *his* emotions. In attempting to gain impossible control over him, we give him the power to control our inner and exterior lives.

The belief that we were somehow inferior or "bad" people when we were children compels us to repeat the past and master it, this time attempting to do it right. In the process we become super-nurturers, trying to fix other people's lives, please them and take care of them. If we just try harder and find the magical formula to make him happy, he'll stop being so angry at us or distant from us. If we only find the key, he'll be able to provide all the love and nurturing our parents never gave us. We may find it difficult to admit, but our very selflessness is a covert attempt to control him. It has such a high price, an impossible price.

When we admit powerlessness over the emotional abuse and the emotional abuser, we are finally able give up our hidden and unreasonable expectation that he can or should with a kiss or kind words miraculously heal our childhood wounds. No other person can ever go back and undo the childhood pain which was inflicted on us. No matter how hard the men in our lives try, they cannot be our fathers. We can also give up the secret hope that if this relationship doesn't work out, we'll find the prince/ magician who will heal us next time. We know that we are the only people with power to heal ourselves.

The self-defeating patterns of thinking and acting we learned when we were young are reinforced by a culture firmly convinced that the next how-to-save-your-marriage article in a women's magazine will provide the ultimate clue to a happily-ever-after relationship. We're bombarded on all sides with suggestions on how to manipulate men into loving us more and behaving the way we'd like them to, from cooking them gourmet meals to trying the latest sex technique on them. Expert cooking and sex may impress men, but they don't cause men to love us, be sexually faithful to us or treat us with respect. We can't *make* anyone love us without their full cooperation. How much they care or don't care about us is up to them. It is not something we can control. A new shade of eye shadow may improve the way we look, but it won't improve a marriage, no matter what Madison Avenue tells us.

The Martyrdom Trap

Because psychologically abusive men are dependent on us to meet their emotional needs and to express the vulnerable, sensitive sides of themselves, which they're so frantically trying to repress, sometimes we're bound to feel overloaded. The resentment which builds from carrying this double burden enables us to slide easily into the trap of martyrdom. You hate feeling like you must read his mind and meet his needs before he asks. You chafe at enabling him to be irresponsible, unreliable or emotionally cold by rationalizing his behavior, denying it or accepting his unpredictable moods as your fault. Yet you do it while all the time self-denial eats away at you on the inside.

On the surface our martyrdom appears selfless, but underneath it is self-serving and manipulative. Sacrificing our own worth to the men in our lives, allows us to place ourselves on holier-than-thou pedestals. We cash in our self-esteem for halos, which allow us to view ourselves as better than the men we live with. We are sweet, kind, loving, gentle and forgiving.

• When we elect ourselves to sainthood, we turn our backs on our true inner strengths which don't depend on the actions of others in order to shine. To make it possible for you to be a saint, he must be a sinner. If he really did mend his ways, you'd tumble from your pedestal back into the realm of ordinary humanity. Sometimes we subconsciously manipulate situations in our marriages so that we can cling to this position of moral superiority, even though we may tell him and ourselves that we want his behavior to improve.

Using His Anger As An Excuse

Our martyrdom and exclusive focus on controlling our mate's feelings and behavior has yet another pay-off for us. Whether we lack the courage to go back to school, make friends or learn a new skill, we have a tendency to blame it all on him. If it weren't for him, we'd be happy. If it weren't for him, we could take art classes or learn to ski. We could get angry and express it. If we were assertive or joined a club and went to meetings, he'd be hurt or furious. Often women in emotionally abusive relationships, use their husbands as excuses to avoid developing their potentials or feelings and expressing emotions.

As long as we blame him for our own lack of courage, we're protected from facing that lack and from ever taking measures to correct it. When we convince ourselves that we are stagnating for him, we are, in effect, using the emotional abuse as an insurance policy against failure. If we never try anything, we never fail. Again, by trying to manipulate his emotions and behavior, by trying to stay on his good side and spending most of our time analyzing his motives, we give up our power and responsibility for our own lives. We exist in a state of voluntary paralysis.

Our helplessness and self-pity offer still another benefit when we use our partner's psychological and verbal abuse as a way to buy tickets then cash them in by acting out our anger. We use his behavior as the rationalization to drink too much or to overeat. When we're short-tempered with our children, we excuse ourselves because our spouse is so short-tempered with us. His coldness "forces" us into affairs or sexual dysfunction. He's making us take too many pills or shop compulsively. We just can't help ourselves!

The cycle is complete. We're blaming him for our lack of control just as vehemently, albeit silently, as he does us for his own lack of self-control. One of the most difficult things for us to admit is that we and our psychologically abusive mates have a great deal in common. Many times we share dysfunctional family backgrounds. We share the same need to rigidly control others and blame them for our feelings. The one thing we don't share is our method of manipulation. His is overt and outwardly destructive — he is outraged. Ours is passive and self-destructive — we are enraged. To acknowledge our underlying similarities with our mates is to give up the last vestiges of the illusion that we can control their behavior when we're really at the mercy of our own shortcomings.

When we give up our futile attempts to control him and his abusiveness, we can finally come to accept that his emotional outbursts have more to do with him than they do with us and that our pain has more to do with ourselves than it does with him. As long as we try to manage his inner anguish instead of doing something about our own, we will remain frozen in denial and our lives will continue to be unmanageable.

Where His Rage Comes From

It helps us to let go of our desire to control when we understand where he's coming from. Most emotionally abusive men grew up in families where there was never enough love, attention and respect to go around. Often these men had love/hate relationships with their mothers. When they marry us, we become mother replacements. Much of the stored rage they feel is then targeted at us. One part of them, the angry part, wants us to be nothing like Mom and reacts with fury when we do or say anything that triggers a reminder of the past. The rages are his attempt to resolve old hurts. We are recipients for the words he wishes he could have yelled at his mother when he was a little child. Because we are not his mother, and yelling at us is not going to heal his mother wound, no matter how vicious his words and how loud his voice, he is caught in a pattern of repeating the tantrums over and over again to no effect. Because the very fact that we are women is enough to provoke his identification with us as his mother, there is no way short of a sex-change operation to stop the projection until he sees it himself and decides to deal with the emotional issues of his past.

Another part of him, the desperately vulnerable and needy part, craves us to give the nurturance and unconditional love he never had. He feels angry and abandoned when we cannot give them to him. He needs us to play two opposite roles, mother and anti-mother at the same time. Since we can't do this, there is no way we can win. No matter which role we play, he will be angry.

Often women married to psychologically abusive men complain that their husbands or lovers act like big babies. In a sense, they *are* big babies, crying and demanding to be emotionally fed, complaining when they are fed. His needs are insatiable.

"You hurt me. You don't listen to me. If you don't agree with me, you don't love me. You don't validate me." Placating him brings only fleeting peace at best because he's often unsure of his needs.

Walking a tightrope, attempting to control the abuse by striving for perfection and never making a misstep, is nerve-wracking and takes an emotional toll on us. Our anxiety shows, no matter how hard we try to conceal it. It may come out in the bedroom where we have difficulty relaxing and enjoying sex or it may come out in jumpiness. When we cower and cry in response to our angrily aggressive mates, we remind them of their own vulnerability and the verbal attacks often grow more intense than they were to begin with.

We need to remember that we cannot be perfect no matter how hard we try; that the harder we try, the more mistakes we make. We are not the cause of our mate's unhappy childhood and nothing we can do, no amount of love or reassurance or caretaking we can give will undo the past. The seeds of emotional abuse were sown in his psyche long before we ever came on the scene. It is not our fault they were planted. It is neither our responsibility nor within our power to uproot them. He must face his own vulnerabilities and angry defenses. We can't face them for him.

When we stop accepting blame and trying to take control over the abuse, we can detach enough to figure out what's really happening to us and how we feel about it. We can start to understand that although what we did or didn't do may have triggered his angry feelings, it certainly wasn't cause for a terrifying display of temper. His stormy internal climate and the coping behavior he learned early in life are responsible for his rages. Burning the roast or getting it on the table 15 minutes late does not mean that we hate him or that we are deliberately setting out to infuriate him. Neither does it mean we're terrible people. No matter what your spouse may insist, everybody makes mistakes and *not* everybody is punished for them with the equivalent of an atomic bomb.

When we stop the denial, we start to recognize that far from helping him, our attempts to control the emotional abuse and manage our relationship have enabled him to act the way he does. As long as we take responsibility for his feelings and actions, he has no reason to change. We are like the woman who drives her alcoholic husband to the liquor store to buy his bottle so he won't get another DUI. When we no longer play the role of enabler, we make it more difficult for him to comfortably function in the old destructive patterns.

Yes, he may decide to leave you and find another woman who will enable him. That may be a frightening possibility for you to contemplate, but the possibility has always been there even though you didn't acknowledge it. The only person you will never lose or leave is yourself. To think that life is otherwise is only a deceptive illusion and feeds the frantic self-defeating desire to control others.

Paradoxically, giving up the neurotic hope that you can reform him won't cause you to feel hopeless or powerless. On the contrary, it releases you to assess your situation realistically, to make sensible decisions and to focus on the very necessary work of healing yourself. You will learn to lift yourself up, rather than putting yourself down before he does to minimize the painful effects of his insults. You will find other ways to be happy besides a compelling need to be needed — if only for a verbal punching bag. The energy you invested in the hopeless cause of managing, manipulating and controlling is suddenly available for investment in yourself.

The only person I can change is me. I will use the energy released by this new understanding to begin the work of healing myself.

4

Step Two

We came to believe that a power greater than
ourselves could restore us to sanity.

"God hugs you. You are encircled by the arms
of the mystery of God."

Hildegard of Bingen

Before we can admit that a Power greater than ourselves can restore us to sanity, we need to go beyond
viewing our lives as simply unmanageable and confess to
ourselves that our lives and our way of thinking have gone
insane. Having built our perceptions about our relationships on a foundation of denial, such an admission is an
extremely difficult one to make. We're often afraid that by
acknowledging the craziness of our lives, our marriages
will crumble. In truth, whether we care to admit it or not,
emotionally abusive relationships are constructed on shifting sands of negative emotions. We can deny all we want,
but that doesn't change the fact that love, respect and

trust, the essentials for any healthy relationship, are cracked and eroded — perhaps beyond repair.

When we become aware of our relationship insanity, we can no longer remain in the fairly comfortable position of labeling our spouses as the only ones with the problem. True, he does have a problem, but we have two — the emotional abuse and our reaction toward it.

How often have we found ourselves walking on eggs, afraid to say or do anything lest we trigger an explosion? How often have we told the kids they couldn't have friends over because it might disturb Daddy? How often have we put his needs before our own to the point where we lost track of what it was we needed? We have spent sleepless nights trying to figure out how to please him. We have cried ourselves to sleep from loneliness and pain. The dictionary defines sanity as soundness or health of mind. The years we've spent in verbally and emotionally abusive relationships have clearly ravaged our mental health.

Certainly we've found ways to cope with the stresses we face daily, but those coping mechanisms are seldom what could be called healthy. We may have become shopaholics, buying more clothes or household possessions than we'll ever use. We may overeat to fill the empty place inside us or perhaps become anorexic or bulimic to exercise control over our bodies because we feel powerless in any other relationship except for that with food. Some of us drink too much. Others turn to prescription drugs. Some become sexually compulsive, seeking a quick emotional fix in a string of affairs which leave us both physically and emotionally unsatisfied. For others, coping means becoming a workaholic either in a paying job or a volunteer agency. We may become supermoms, focusing all of our time and attention on our children. Once we can take even a half-objective look at our lives, we find it hard to hide from the recognition that we're in pain and that the ways in which we treat ourselves only serve to make the pain worse. They do not reflect a soundness of mind.

Because we may not know any other ways to cope besides the ones we've chosen, we use them compulsively whenever the pain peaks. And since we've given total control over our emotions to another human, we have no say over how much we'll hurt at a given moment. Not only are we addicted to the men we live with, desperately needing them to validate us because we never knew or have forgotten how to affirm and take care of ourselves, we're often addicted to an unworkable coping mechanism we believe we need in order to live with him. Our lives consist of addiction piled upon addiction. We're convinced that without our man's approval and our substance or behavior of choice, we can't survive. We need them to feel whole, to feel normal, to feel alive. "I feel pain, therefore I am" is crazy thinking.

Emotional Terrorism

In effect a woman who lives with a psychological and verbal abuser is living with an emotional terrorist. Her thoughts and feelings bear many of the earmarks of those of the political terrorist's victim. Emotionally abusive men are dominators and subjugators. Even though they may not lock their wives in dark basements or carry machine guns, they share much in common with terrorists. Living with a person who denies your perceptions of reality, who gives mixed messages and is both unpredictable and irrational, causes psychic trauma to the most "together" woman as she changes and rearranges her behavior, thoughts and even her feelings to avoid the punitive mental torture she knows he's capable of dishing out.

Psychologists, who specialize in the treatment of hostage victims, report that captives undergo several distinct phases as they adjust to their status as victims. Although those of us who have lived in abusive relationships were physically free to walk away, we nonetheless allowed ourselves to be held emotional hostage because we believed that no other man, except for the abuser, would tolerate a relationship with us, that we deserved the abuse or that the abusive relationship was normal.

The first stage of captivity is emotion numbing denial: This really can't be happening. How many times have we told ourselves that the men who love us really can't be yelling obscenities at us, calling us whores, flaunting affairs or threatening to kill us? In the denial stage we forget everything we've learned about how to function as happy, healthy adults. We expend our total energy on survival. For a woman in a psychologically abusive relationship this means being obedient and trying to anticipate her partner's needs and meet them without being asked. It means not crossing him and doing everything within her power to avoid his wrath and subsequent punishment.

Some women who are highly capable and competent in other areas of their lives become "helpless" when the front door closes and they are alone with their mates because the sum total of their energy is expended on surviving within the relationship. They deny their strengths and good qualities, shrugging off their effective coping mechanisms, much as they might a coat when they come inside the emotionally abusive house. Others who grew up in dysfunctional homes never learned mature coping skills. They left the psychological prison of one dysfunctional family for another, this time with their partner as jailer. The more our psychic and physical lives are in danger, the less concerned we become about such luxuries as happiness and self-esteem. We lose perspective and our thinking becomes distorted and confused as we get by on a day-to-day (and sometimes a minute-to-minute) basis.

Quickly we learn that if we are to keep our marriages, we must go a step further beyond self-protection and ingratiate ourselves to our emotionally abusive mates. Once we begin to ingratiate, we become grateful to the men we allow to have power over us for the instances when they don't misuse it. We tell ourselves that we're happy they don't beat us. We read the newspapers and tell ourselves we're lucky that, although he has a short fuse and blows up a lot, he hasn't killed us or he doesn't drink or he at least has a job. Like political hostages we instinctively reduce ourselves to a state of psychological infancy and become dependent on our captors for sustenance. While many of us work and rely on our mates only for psychological survival, some of us depend on the men we live with to support us. If we've not been in the workplace for years and have children, leaving can become a terrifying option, one we don't ever consider.

The Stockholm Syndrome

Gratitude, even when it's not well founded, forms strong bonds between women and the men who abuse them. In the field of terrorism, those bonds are called the *Stockholm Syndrome* after a woman held hostage in a Swedish bank robbery who fell in love with her captor and married him. As do many hostages, we form a deep fantasy bond with the abuser, the more dependent on him we become and the more severe the emotional abuse, the greater is our need to make him out to be a hero. Some of us rationalize our man's outrageous behavior, explaining it away or even blocking it from our consciousness. Many emotionally abused women grow furious when they hear from a friend or therapist that they should consider leaving an abusive partner. Even talk of women's liberation is enough to anger them. Emotionally overwhelming circumstances of their lives literally turn their thinking upside down so they are incensed at their liberators and enamored of those who have tormented them.

Certainly the ways in which hostages adapt to life-threatening situations are methods to insure their greater chances of survival. A prisoner of war who repeatedly tries to escape will, no doubt, be shot. A kidnap victim who rages aloud at her abductors will be silenced. A woman who is physically battered, or whose mate threatens her with a weapon, would be a fool to vehemently try to talk sense into him — her main concern is for her physical safety. She needs to quickly and without fanfare remove herself from the dangerous situation. At least giving the appearance of compliance in these instances is adaptive.

On the other hand, women who allow themselves to be
emotionally battered are usually not in life-or-death situations. Such a woman hands her paycheck over to her
out-of-work husband who gambles. He loses and she and
her children go without food. Next time she's paid, she
hands the check over to him again, afraid he'll leave her or
have an affair as he's threatened if she doesn't. Her fears
of the consequences of abandonment and rejection are
overblown, so she feels required to pay an extremely high
price (and force her children to pay one) to avoid the
imagined results of her husband's possible departure. She
does not take steps to change the relationship or to leave
it because she maintains an illusion that she is dependent
on her mate. Her compliance is maladaptive and unhealthy
because it is not based in reality. Her life is insane, and no
matter how often she blames her husband for her troubles, she cooperates with him fully in the craziness that is
their marriage.

Cyclical Warfare

Because abuse is chronic and cyclical, the life of a
woman in an emotionally battering relationship resembles
psychological warfare. Even when there appears to be
peace, it is only temporary because the very ground of
her relationship is studded with buried land mines —
ones she didn't plant and often can't detect before she
triggers one and it blows up in her face. She becomes
wary and timid before the explosion she is sure will come
but unsure of when or why. During a pitched battle,
which she knows she will lose, she may disassociate,
running on automatic much like a soldier on the battle-
field. Afterward she feels grateful toward her spouse for
stopping the attack, and her self-esteem is left in tattered
shreds as she once again cautiously treks across the mine
field hoping to avoid further trouble.

It is no wonder she develops battle fatigue from the
constant struggle for survival in the conflict situation
that is her relationship. Once her marriage becomes a
perpetual battleground with no permanent truce in sight,

she becomes physically exhausted, mentally drained, emotionally ragged and spiritually weary.

When life is a battle, we begin to experience unexplained stomachaches and other physical complaints. Our mental and emotional burnout clouds our thinking and makes it impossible to take rational steps to solve our problem. The spiritual weariness convinces us that life has no meaning and that there is no hope for us. Because of the situational stressors we face, we become temporarily insane.

Post-Traumatic Stress Syndrome

Women who grew up in chemically dependent families, or who were incested or abused in other ways, may suffer in addition from post-traumatic stress syndrome, the same emotional malady psychologists have found in Vietnam War veterans. When our childhoods were traumatic, we carried the memory of them deep inside of us, even though we may have erased the horrors from our conscious minds or think we have dealt with them rationally. Like veterans, we may at times feel unaccountably depressed, enraged or self-destructive in response to our memories, even though we truly believe we are reacting to what is currently happening in our lives. Like veterans, we have flashbacks — feelings and images of our previous trauma (in our case of abuse or abandonment) which are triggered by similar events in the present.

While war veterans may flash back when an alarm clock sounds or a fire engine passes, our triggers can be a loud angry voice, threats to leave us or particular words that we heard as children. Certain rooms in our houses may be more potent for us than others, as well as certain times of day and certain circumstances. In the midst of a flashback, we react to what happened to us as children, helpless to stop the abuse and completely dependent on our parents, rather than as adults who can choose to leave the room or leave the relationship and still survive. Operating in the midst of an extremely powerful illusion, we cannot think or act rationally, no

matter how hard we try. We've carried a form of situational insanity with us into our relationships.

Once we face our off-the-wall ways of relating to our
spouses and ourselves, we may find we're even more
vulnerable to his blame game. We're used to taking on
responsibility for the abuser's thoughts, feelings and actions, so now when we hear him accuse us of driving him
crazy, that we're the sick ones, it may feel like a double
whammy, especially if we carried the same labels as children. Admitting that we're living insane lives isn't the
same thing as accepting responsibility for his craziness.
Allowing ourselves to feel and act emotionally unbalanced,
just because he or someone else says we are, isn't a
healthy autonomous style of relating — it's crazy.

When we are defined as sick, without thinking we tend
to conform to fit the labels and act out the roles we've
been assigned in our relationships. It's a matter of a self-
fulfilling prophecy coming true. Our conditioning makes
us vulnerable for this type of insane thought process. As
teenagers we're taught to take care of men. We're told
that we're responsible for the relationship. We also learn
that women in general are flaky. When we live in a
woman-hating society, it's easy to internalize the notion
that just by being female we're somehow inferior and
sick. We're too sensitive, too emotional. Men are the
leaders and the rational ones. When we live with a
woman-hating man, we're doubly damned. He may be
screaming bloody murder and throwing things, but when
he tells us that he had logical reasons for doing this and
we were a basket case for being five minutes late, he's
tapping into years of conditioning.

Typically the emotional abuse we experience is gov-
erned by our spouse's internal cycles. Our relationship
with him is like a roller-coaster ride accelerating faster
and faster. Over time the cycles speed up, growing more
intense — our highs are higher, our lows, lower. At the
same time that we try to meet his unfulfillable needs, we
learn nobody will fill ours so we ignore them. We tell

ourselves we shouldn't feel anything, we shouldn't expect anything, we don't deserve anything. That's crazier still.

The Blame Game

We may try to play the blame game ourselves in an attempt to slide out from the crushing reality we face. It's all his fault our lives are messed up. He's driving *us* crazy, isn't he? The answer to this question is that although his behavior may be crazy-making because it contains so many mixed messages and is so unpredictable, *we* are the ones who tolerate it. No one forced us to involve ourselves in a relationship. No one forced us to accept the emotional abuse as our due and even take responsibility for it. And no one is forcing us now to tolerate the status quo or to remain in the relationship the way it is.

Certainly, he may very well be crazy. At times he acts completely bananas. We can do nothing about his insane way of relating to himself, to us or to the world. We can do something about our own emotional state — *if* we accept that our emotional state isn't rational and if we take responsibility for that rather than blaming it on him.

To understand how little sense denial makes, step out of your own situation for a moment and imagine you are a stranger assessing your current life. You see a woman convinced that she can magically control the feelings and behaviors of another adult as if she were a puppet master and held the strings. At the same time, she allows her puppet to magically pull her emotional strings. You sense her sadness and you hear her crying herself to sleep, yet she tells you she's feeling fine, and there's a false smile perpetually on her face. You sense her anger at the insults and threats she constantly hears, but you see that she's always ready to listen to them. When you tell her she can try to change her behavior, and that if the relationship does not improve, she can leave it, she replies that she is helpless. It isn't all that bad and, besides, at least her husband doesn't beat her. He just has an odd way of showing his affection for her. If he didn't care, he wouldn't abuse her so much. She denies and distorts her perceptions so that she can live in a fantasy world, more tolerable than the real world. Chances are you'd conclude this woman was thinking and living like a madwoman. She is. You are. Emotionally abused wives lead twisted lives. That reality is inescapable.

After the veil of denial is removed from our eyes and we finally get a clear vision of the way we've been living, the evidence for insanity can be overwhelming to deal with. We finally see that our denial, itself, was crazy.

Perhaps even before you started reading this book, you already suspected your relationship was haywire and your reactions were far from healthy and balanced. That awareness doesn't automatically erase feelings of shame, guilt, sadness and anger. Once we start looking at the pieces of our lives and our wounded self-esteem, we often feel more off center than we did when we could cling to the admittedly elusive mirage of sanity. The task of restoring our emotional well-being is simply too enormous and complex for us to handle on our own. This is why the Second Step asks that we believe a Power greater than ourselves can provide us with the inner calm we so desperately lack.

Turning It Over

Believing that there is Something outside of ourselves, which is stronger than us, provides a way to experience the love and healing we didn't get in childhood, the love and comfort we so anxiously sought but didn't find in relationships with men. Although we possess numerous talents and strong inner resources, we cannot mend our hurt successfully without outside help. We have struggled alone to find fulfillment in abusive relationships. It didn't work. The testimony of our failure lies in the current insanity of our lives.

The Second Step demands that we risk a leap of faith, that we trust in the benevolence of this Higher Power. We move beyond the egotistical pseudo-independence so many of us have adopted as a defense against our inner feelings of betrayal, admitting that there is a Force bigger and more powerful than ourselves or any other human

and that we need help from that Power. This faith provides the missing piece we're lacking in our quest for
inner peace.

Some of us are turned off to religion. Others have
never really considered spirituality. In abusive homes spirituality is either ignored because there's no time for it or
it's used as a weapon. Some have never searched inside to
discover what we believed. We let our husbands and our
fathers define our spirituality and our values systems,
tailoring the expression of our faith to match what we
thought was expected of us. When we lived with men
who told us we had to think their way or else, we had to
put spirituality on the back burner. It was one of those
issues we planned to deal with sometime in the future.

Those of us who didn't believe in a Higher Power or
never even considered the question, had no source of help
or strength except for what we could give to ourselves.
We often felt terribly alone, a spiritual isolation that left
us disconnected and empty.

Belief in a Power greater than ourselves enables us to
take one day at a time in our relationships. When we have
faith that this Power is good and has the ability to heal us,
we can stop carrying our burden alone. We begin to
experience the unconditional love we needed, but didn't
get as children, and that is impossible for us to get as
adults from other adults or from our own children. Once
we stop our constant struggle, once we let go and let
God, we can catch our breath. Relaxed and renewed, we
find that our healing journey isn't the grueling uphill
battle we feared.

Finding Our Faith

At this stage problems with belief in a Higher Power
aren't unusual. Even though we may want to believe, we
have serious doubts that we're on the right path because
we aren't experiencing breath-taking revelations or an
overwhelming sense of peacefulness. We turn to religious
teachings without understanding that many religious
writers and leaders haven't experienced the same crisis of

faith we have. They write and talk about what they know. Their life experiences may not necessarily apply in every instance to our lives.

When we grow discouraged and find our faith in a Higher Power slipping, we need to reread Step Two, paying careful attention to the words "came to believe." Those three words imply slow growth of faith, rather than sudden dramatic insight complete with flashing lights, angelic choruses and the scent of incense. In truth, many extremely spiritual people wrestle with questions of faith, their belief isn't easy for them either. They come to it in a series of baby steps, not one gigantic leap. For most of us there is no blinding light or profound breathtaking insight.

We grow day by day to know our Higher Power better as manifested through nature and in our own thoughts and hearts. We see It manifested in the kindnesses others do for us and in our own welling up of love. Some days the benevolent Force is more noticeable than others. In the doubting times we learn to operate "as if" we were secure in the knowledge of the Presence in our lives. Just because we temporarily cannot or do not acknowledge a Force more powerful than ourselves, does not mean our Higher Power doesn't exist or doesn't care for us. It indicates we need to slow down and open ourselves more fully.

I will open myself to the possibility of a Higher Power who loves me even when I do not love myself and who gives balance and peace to my life.

5

Step Three

We made a decision to turn our will and our lives over
to the care of God as we understood God.

*"Joy fixes us to eternity and pain fixes us to time.
But desire and fear hold us in bondage to time;
detachment breaks the bond."*

Simone Weil
The New York Notebook

Many women involved in emotionally abusive relationships feel Step Three, detaching from the desires and fears
which hold us in bondage, is like jumping out of the frying
pan and into the fire. Our lives have taught us that we can
trust no one, and we often cling desperately to illusions of
complete self-control as the solution to our problems.

Because of our past relationships with our fathers and
our more recent relationships with men, our image of the
traditional male God is usually an unpleasant one. He's
the supreme masculine authority figure, and we've
learned from bitter experience that men aren't about to

look out for our best interests. Because our mothers may have failed us and because we lack faith in ourselves, we may find belief and trust in a female Goddess Principle equally threatening.

It is safer to conceptualize a Prime Cosmic Force, which created the world then lost interest and is now inaccessible, than to believe in a God or Goddess with whom we can have a personal and intimate relationship. From our experiences we may have come to believe that warm, loving relationships are fraught with peril and may be an impossible dream. Now we're asked to trust our will and our lives to the care of a Supreme Being, the most intimate and vulnerable relationship possible. We may admit that there truly exists a Power greater than ourselves, but how can we ever turn our will and lives over to Him, Her or It? For that matter, *why* should we?

The Search For The Cosmic Answer

From the beginning of humanity women and men have looked outside themselves for a Divine Source to explain creation, their purpose in being and the events of their lives. Throughout history this search for a Cosmic Answer has taken many forms, all springing from a craving to know a Higher Power, expressing a need which many theologians and psychologists believe is as much a human requirement for survival as food, air or water. Whether people think of their Higher Power as a Mother Goddess, a Heavenly Patriarch or an androgynous Universal Creative Force, the notion that there is Something out there, which is wiser, more powerful than we are, is part of our human heritage.

No matter how strongly we wish to deny it, we are spiritual in nature. As the only creatures on earth who are aware that we are born of mothers and know that eventually we will die as everyone does, we seek to find patterns in our lives and purpose for them. We can look to biomedical science to explain the mysteries of DNA and to psychology and social sciences to tell us how our personalities have evolved and to predict how we will act in a given situation. But medicine, psychology and even physics cannot explain the ultimate meaning of life, nor do they pretend to. The meaning of life is a spiritual question and will not be satisfied with less than spiritual answers.

The first commandment of the famous Ten of the Judeo-Christian tradition states: "Thou shalt have no other gods before me." Here the Supreme Being instructs us that our spirituality, the seeking of the Ultimate Principle and Reality must come first in our priorities. Earlier matriarchal belief systems also stressed that the Goddess was not to be ignored. Eastern religious teaching, as well, instructs that our relationship with the Sacred should be the most important in our lives. If the pieces of the puzzle of our lives are to fall into place, we must first pay attention to the glue which holds them together — our Higher Power.

In our day-to-day existence, first in dysfunctional families then enmeshed in relationships with emotionally abusive men, we've learned to set other human beings up as tin gods and to sacrifice ourselves to them. In addition, we may have set up other idols for ourselves in the form of alcohol, drugs, chocolate chip cookies, work or the local shopping mall. Some of us have deified our children, pouring every ounce of ourselves into their lives and obsessing on their happiness. Our spirituality, the sense of connectedness with a Higher Power, has taken a minor role amid the clutter of our lives — if it has any place at all. It is no wonder that we feel unsatisfied and incomplete.

Not only have we given other people and things a more major role than the Divine Force outside ourselves, we've placed ourselves in that position as well. Every time we said, "It's all my fault," whether it was in response to our parents' divorce or our husband's outrage, we've set ourselves up as gods who have control over other people's emotions and actions. Every time we automatically say, "I'm sorry," in response to our child's anger, our husband's pain at his childhood or, in some cases, natural disasters within a hundred-mile radius, we do the same. This notion is a very negative one, but it's a powerful one as well.

The Second Step asked us to cease trying to play God
and to stop colluding with our partner's grandiose attempts
to do the same in order to create a space for our Higher
Power to enter our lives. Unless we've done the necessary
spiritual housecleaning implicit in the Second Step and
have rid ourselves of the notion that we have godlike
dominion over others or that others have godlike dominion
over us, our relationship with our Higher Power will be
superficial at best and at worst, a spiritual power struggle.

The Paradox Of Surrender

Many of us resist taking the Third Step to recovery for
this very reason. We feel that just when we're getting in
touch with our core, learning to take control of our lives,
we must surrender ourselves, literally give away our wills
— to another Patriarch if we're of the Judeo-Christian
tradition. It doesn't make sense that to be independent, we
need to depend on God. Because we've grown so accustomed to defending ourselves against the power plays of
others and because we've been so obsessed with gaining
control over their emotions and actions, we're well primed
for this power struggle with the Supreme Being.

The paradox of trusting our Higher Power enough to
surrender our wills and our lives is that the more dependent
we become on the Divine for love, nurturance and guidance,
the more independent we become in our relationships with
others. We no longer have to look to other people, including
our abusive partners, for approval and validation of our
self-worth. Our Higher Power thought we were worthy
enough to create us, and believes us worthy enough to
intervene in our lives today. Working as a team with our
Supreme Being, we have a strength of purpose, a content-
ment and a solidity that our own will power cannot bring
us. By shifting our focus outside of ourselves and allowing
our spiritual faculties to bloom, we become more aware of
ourselves than we've ever been before.

Often we express a longing to be able to trust and to be
trusted. A word we might substitute for trust is faith.
That longing is nothing more than words until we put it

into practice. When we surrender to a Higher Power, we are making the ultimate act of faith. In truth the Supreme Being isn't only the most logical starting point for trust, It is the safest as well. Even though we may have told ourselves that we'd never trust anybody ever again, we can still trust God/dess because He/She isn't a body — He/She is pure power, absolute truth.

Religion As A Weapon

Women who grew up in dysfunctional families have an especially difficult time believing in a benevolent Power, especially if our parents used God as a weapon to shame us or as a justification for their abuse or neglect. If God sanctioned what happened in our families, we want no part of Him.

Most people do profess to adhere to some religion. Unfortunately many don't often practice what the belief system to which they pay lip service preaches. Social workers and psychologists are finding that child abuse, physical, emotional and sexual, often occurs in strict religious homes.

In addition the family rules, which may have been well-meaning but were extremely rigid, can constitute a form of spiritual abuse. When we grow up in such families, we learn to live with perpetual shame for our very normal feelings and thoughts, as well as for actions which are a natural part of our development process. As we grow older, we may feel deep shame for even being alive, believing we are sinful worms in the sight of God. We are taught that to have self-esteem is as wicked as is having too much fun. We are tutored to despise our bodies and to not only honor, but obey our parents no matter what they do.

Such an upbringing can have the effect of spiritual rape or battery. Our very souls are assaulted, subdued and invaded. It is no wonder we may spend a good part of our adult lives running from any form of spirituality. In effect, our parents may have robbed us of the chance to explore a fulfilling essential side of ourselves, *if* we continue as adults to react to their teachings, rather than to act on our own and learn for ourselves what our spirituality is all about.

The Third Step says we are to surrender our will and our lives to God *as we know God*, not God as our parents knew Him or God as the people down the street know God or even as our husbands know Him. This step gives many of us our first opportunity as adults to discover what we believe about a Supreme Being. We have a chance to take out our old beliefs, dust them off and examine them, deciding whether to keep them, toss them out altogether and substitute new ones for the old or revise them so that they fit our lives now. The wording of the Third Step is purposefully vague, not necessarily out of fear of offending people, but to enable us to do the work of defining our Higher Power for ourselves.

If when we were younger, the Supreme Being was used against us as a weapon, someone who would get us if we didn't keep the family secrets or if we exercised emotional independence from our parents, chances are we see Him as a punitive and unforgiving parent figure now. On the other hand, if we were taught that we would break His heart if we disobeyed our parents, we learned to see Him as a guilt-tripper. If one of our parents was an alcoholic or an abuser, we may have developed a great deal of anger at this all-powerful God for not saving us. We may still be furious at our Higher Power.

That rage is natural to feel. It's natural to express. Our Higher Power isn't chained by the insecurities and fears of our fathers or our husbands or boyfriends. God is bigger than that, compassionate and understanding; big enough to hear our anger and outrage at what happened, big enough to heal it. Our Higher Power doesn't whine, "If you loved me, you'd keep your mouth shut," or "If you admit your true feelings, I'll zap you with a lightning bolt." Our anger at Fate or the Supreme Being can be a starting point for spiritual growth.

We stagnate spiritually when we deny our outrage and fall into the magical thinking of our childhood, deciding

that if we choose to ignore the presence of a Supreme
Being, if we choose not to give It the satisfaction of acknowledgment, then It won't exist. Refusing to deal with
the issue of a Higher Power may be an effective, temporary defense, but denial doesn't make our Higher Power
go away, just as denying our childhood pain doesn't make
that go away, just as telling ourselves it isn't raining and
leaving the umbrella at home, won't keep us dry. Our
Higher Power is at work in our lives at all times.

When we acknowledge that, we can be in harmony with
the Supreme Being and our lives will flow with more ease.
When we deny the existence of a Force beyond ourselves,
our lives become an inharmonious struggle filled with
discordant, jarring notes and self-created difficulties.

How do we begin to know the God or Goddess Principle
on a deep and mature level, so that our lives have richer
meaning? Before we can go beyond them, we need to
delve into our earliest images of the Higher Power.

The Patriarchal God

According to J. B. Phillips, a theologian and translator of
the New Testament, as children we tend to model our
concept of God after our fathers. (We model Grace or the
Holy Spirit after our mothers.) That's logical. In prayers,
hymns and in the Bible, God is referred to as the Father.
When we envision Him, we may see a Higher Power who
doesn't know we exist, one who certainly would never take
a personal interest in our lives if we grew up with a father
who was cold and withdrawn. For us God is a disinterested
if dignified old white-bearded man who sits on a throne. If
our fathers neglected us, we can't even begin to imagine a
god who will care for us. Those of us who lived with
fathers who made and broke promises may view God as
Somebody who is out to trick us, Someone who lays traps
and then is infuriated when we step into them. If our
father was angry and abusive, we attribute those qualities
to God, determining that He's arbitrary and punitive.

Later life experiences with an emotionally abusive man,
who we set up as a household deity and sacrificed our-

selves to, adds to the layer of negative feelings we have about a Higher Power. The man in our lives says we've sinned and constantly condemns us for it. And that's what God does, doesn't He? We learn from growing up in dysfunctional homes and from living in them as adults to believe we don't deserve love. A Higher Power who can love us without strings, in spite of our flaws, can be unimaginable to us.

When we stop to think about it, we may have been fleeing from the wrath of God most of our adult lives, hiding because we think He's out to get us. We tend to mold our image of the Higher Power out of the raw material of our fathers, our boyfriends and our husbands. When we seek a relationship with the Divine, we may use the same ineffective and self-defeating behaviors we do in dealing with them.

We may debase ourselves and deform our beingness in an attempt to please God, forgetting that our Higher Power created us in the first place, and so must essentially be happy with us. Certainly we may have to make changes in our ways in order to be attuned to the Divine, but we are not asked to become entirely different than who we are, and in effect, re-invent ourselves. When we put ourselves down, we are degrading our Higher Power's creation.

We may beg, wheedle, whine and cajole God, because we learned that's what our father expected and believe that is what our partner expects. Since we learned to bargain in our earthbound relationships, we might try to bargain with our Higher Power — if You just get me through today, I'll give money to charity and stop using swear words when I'm angry. Once we realize that our Higher Power is a source of unconditional love, caring without strings, such tactics are patently ridiculous.

On the other hand, we may spin fantasies of a Higher Power which are mirror-reversals of our negative experience of a father figure. The Supreme Being for us becomes a divine sugar daddy or a cosmic Santa Claus who will indulge our every whim, no matter what the cost or consequence to other people. We spend our time making up lists of demands and become enraged when they aren't met immediately. We forget that our Higher Power is the ultimate wisdom and truth and that He or She may know more about what we really need at a given time then we, with our limited perspective, do.

Our Higher Power is not simply a clone of our father. Neither is our Higher Power necessarily the exact opposite of our father. When we work to free ourselves of preconceived notions of what a Supreme Being should be and open ourselves to the myriad possibilities of what a Supreme Being could be, we can truly apprehend That Which Is.

Unfortunately, many of us run from the quiet contemplation which is the most effective way to develop a deep relationship with the Ultimate Spiritual Presence. We scurry around performing good deeds. When we finally settle down to spend time on our relationship with our Higher Power, we only do it with a book on our lap or a sermon on the TV. Doing good is important as is studying and learning, but the route to an intimate relationship with our Creator is to slow down and listen to what that Creator has to tell us.

Organized Religion — Does It Help?

While some of us find that our spiritual practice has been enhanced and focused by organized worship, other women involved in emotionally abusive relationships may not have been helped by the church experience. Some have been turned off by the condescending pity and lack of understanding they received when they openly shared their personal experiences. Self-righteousness and judgmental attitudes from people who profess to be religious can also turn a woman away from her spiritual path if she doesn't realize that the narrow minds of some churchgoers say more about themselves than they do about the Higher Power.

Suffer now, so you'll have pie in the sky later attitudes can have an especially negative impact on women who have been emotionally or physically battered. In some

cases we've been counseled by ministers to put up with
the abuse our husbands dished out. Battered women who
seek religious counseling typically stay in abusive relationships longer than do women who don't. When we
encounter attitudes and teachings which run counter to
our inner voice, we need to remind ourselves that our
relationship with our Higher Power can be fostered by
organized worship and fellowship with other believers,
but at its heart, it is a very individual matter. If a particular church or spiritual group impacts our lives in a destructive manner, we must gather the courage to leave
and seek fellowship elsewhere.

Our search for the Higher Power can take many different pathways. Some women find a sense of spiritual support from the traditions in which they were raised.
Others turn to Eastern meditative traditions. Still others
find peace and abiding serenity by placing their trust in a
female deity. For many women, the concept of a Higher
Power needs no gender personification in order to be real.
They conceive of a Supreme Being who is energy or light.

Finding Our Inner Wisdom

No matter how we come to view our Higher Power, once
we open ourselves to that Power and allow It to flow inside
of us so that we become spirit-filled, we develop an innate
knowingness that our God/dess is forgiving. That experience of acceptance, unconditional love and complete forgiveness lets us learn to forgive ourselves. The Supreme
Being demands nothing but our acknowledgment, trust
and love. When we surrender our lives and the willfullness
which is actually our feeble attempt to be our own gods, we
become willing to allow God/dess or the All That Is to
direct us. Walking on the right path will follow naturally.

Having placed our trust in our Higher Power, we ready
ourselves to give up our crutch of denial once and for all
and begin the dance of life. Because the Supreme Being is
omnipotent, that means He or She knows everything we
think and feel and do. It is futile to lie to ourselves or to

lie to our Higher Power, so our self-deception and the masks we wear for the world are no longer of use.

Our relationship with the Divine can serve as a model of what open and honest loving human relationships can be. By forming a right relationship with our Higher Power, by trusting and learning that our trust is well founded, we begin to heal our inner wounds and break old habits. We can learn to trust, to love fully. We can open ourselves to the possibility of receiving love and to being convinced that, yes, we do deserve love. The more we practice relating to our Higher Power, the more loving and lovable we feel in our relationships with other people.

What does the Higher Power expect of us in return? Only that we get up one more time than we fall down. Although we surrender to a Force outside of ourselves, we do not give up our essence or our self-esteem. "Love thy neighbor as thyself," means just what it says. In fact, our Higher Power expects us to have a healthy self-respect and then to use that as a base for reaching out to others. Turning our lives and wills over to a Power greater than ourselves doesn't make us doormats; it opens us to being the best we can be. It doesn't take away our freedom of choice; belief expands our options.

I have complete trust in my Higher Power who cares for me and who takes care of me. Today I will let go and let God.

6

Step Four — Part I

We made a searching and fearless moral inventory of ourselves.

"We do not grow absolutely, chronologically.
We grow sometimes in one dimension,
and not in another, unevenly.
We grow partially. We are relative.
We are mature in one realm and childish in
another. The past, present and future
mingle and pull us backward, forward or fix
us in the present. We are made up of
layers, cells, constellations."

Anais Nin

Step Four requires that we take a look at what's happening inside of ourselves and at how those internal states affect us and the other people we encounter. To examine our emotions and attitudes and how we play them out in our daily lives, we can use our intuition (inner-teaching), the small still voice which resides in every one of us. We need to take quiet time alone, time when we are relaxed and can calmly focus in on ourselves without external distractions. In order to hear, we need to listen.

Internal distractions, too, can prevent us from doing the work of the Fourth Step. If, when you begin your inventory, you find yourself obsessing about what to fix for dinner, how to pay your rent or whether or not to color your hair, you may not be ready for the inventory-taking stage of your recovery.

To get unstuck take a few minutes to ask the part of yourself which is blocking this self-examination to identify herself and tell you why she's attempting to halt the process. Possibly your work on the first three steps isn't complete and you'll need to temporarily retreat from the inventory and lay more solid groundwork for it.

When we read the words "fearless" and "searching," we may incorrectly assume that our moral inventory will be a negative one, that we'll study ourselves and our patterns of relating objectively only to find that we're all messed up. The opposite is true for many women recovering from emotionally abusive relationships when they make their self-assessments. As we list our strong points and our weaknesses, we tend to find that we're better people than we initially believed. While we may have an extreme degree of difficulty forming healthy relationships with men, we may shine in our friendships with women or our relationships in the workplace. Our most bothersome character flaws are counterbalanced by some wonderful traits.

Because we've grown up in environments where our positive attributes may have been overlooked while our negative characteristics were constantly criticized, because we formed intimate relationships with men who played the same put-down game, we may, in fact, have a more difficult time accepting the beautiful things about ourselves than we do the ugly. If we are honest in recognizing them, our strengths can be even more frightening to some of us than our weaknesses because they disturb the images we have of ourselves as bad, weak and helpless people.

This confusing rejection of the best inside of us, is an attempt to resolve what psychologists call *cognitive dissonance*, the refusal to accept information which contradicts our long-held beliefs. We view ourselves and the world through a dingy filter rather than through rose-colored glasses. Those of us who tend to minimize and discount our positive qualities will need to search hard and fearlessly acknowledge them when we find them.

On the other hand, some of us defend so strongly against external criticism, we have a difficult time with self-criticism. We have such a shaky sense of self-worth that we deeply believe to admit any flaw, even the most minor one, damns us to doom and threatens our very existence. We've learned to defend ourselves from outside attack by striving for perfection and we adhere to all-or-nothing thinking when we contemplate ourselves. We are either excellent human beings or horrible ones who shouldn't have a right to be alive. For us there is no middle ground.

If it is done well, a moral inventory is a difficult thing to accomplish. It is hard work to detach from ourselves enough to observe our inner and outer workings objectively, rather than through judgmental filters, but we can use those filters as part of our self-analysis, noting them and beginning to observe how they shade our thinking. As we proceed through the stages of inventory we may find ourselves unable to take off our familiar put-down filter or our perfectionistic filter. That should indicate to us that we need to take a break for a time, then come back to our inventory when our energy is renewed. Our "inner eyes" can grow tired and strained just as our physical eyes do when we focus for too long.

Because we're so accustomed to reading other peoples' emotions and needs, we may find it strange and awkward at first to pay so much attention to our own. Initially we may feel silly, self-centered or frivolous when we sit down and attempt to assess just what it is we feel and just where we are at this point in our lives.

Since our lives have been structured around doing things for others, we've become human doings rather than human beings. Using this time and energy on ourselves to take inventory is a first step toward human-beingness. If we persist in taking time to center in on ourselves and to become grounded with who we are, in time we overcome our reluctance to know ourselves, and our alone time becomes enjoyable.

The more time we spend focusing inward and the more careful attention we pay to what we observe there, the more we will learn about who we are. Inventories aren't supposed to be taken in one evening unless you can hire a team of part-time helpers with computer scanners like stores do. Hiring outside help defeats the purpose of self-inventory anyway. Even when you have a therapist and a support group, Fourth-Step self-analysis is a solo job.

Practitioners of Tai Chi, the Oriental movement-oriented meditation, have a gesture which they call embracing the tiger. It symbolizes our need to embrace the clawed, fanged and squirming parts of ourselves, to acknowledge them fully and to love our whole selves, the good and the bad parts. When we refuse to see our demons or to give them validity, they cling to us more tightly. Paradoxically, once we've acknowledged their presence and influence in our lives, once we're able to give them a nonjudgmental embrace, they are more willing to allow us to control our own lives rather than calling all the shots for us. Since our emotions form the base for our attitudes about life and our actions, they are the first tigers we'll acknowledge and embrace. Emotions are part of the human condition. Our task isn't to free ourselves of all emotions; that would be as undesirable as it is impossible. Instead we need to work toward knowing what we're feeling when we're feeling it. That can be tough if we were taught to be ashamed of our feelings, learned never to admit our emotions (except for love and gratitude).

Once we can determine what we're feeling, we're able to notice how balanced or unbalanced our emotional state is. Some of us have a favorite emotion, be it anger, sadness, fear or guilt, which is always present and colors our beliefs about the world. If we're unaware of that constant emotional backdrop, we can't very well do anything about it.

By the same token, some will find that we are very capable of being forgiving, but we don't get angry, even when the situation warrants it. This discovery can be an effective tool for developing more assertiveness.

The following exercises are not by any means all-encompassing. You may wish as you do them, to add or invent some of your own. Because you are a unique individual, your personal inventory is your own. If you allow yourself to be in touch with that quiet voice within, you'll know when you're being honest with yourself and you'll know when you're being dishonest.

Remember that a Fourth-Step inventory is not a pass/fail proposition. No matter what you discover about yourself, you can't flunk your inventory — unless you decide to avoid taking it by inventing phony, self-serving answers. Remember, too, that your inventory is an assessment of who you are at this particular moment in time, not who you were or who you want to be or even who you think you ought to be. To take inventory is to realistically record what is. It is a starting point, not a test or a trial.

Anger/Calm

Anger can be a very useful emotion. It is a fuel for change, giving us the motivation and the energy to make improvements in our lives. Anger is a way we set boundaries. If we never felt irritated or put-upon, we'd never say no. When we honestly acknowledge our anger, we can choose to express it or defuse it. If we never allow ourselves to feel anger or try to deny it we turn anger inward — feeling as if something is eating at us.

On the other hand, when we exist in a constant state of irritation, we may live with the premise of getting even with other people for past hurts inflicted upon us, even when the target of our anger at any given moment wasn't the one who caused us pain. When rage becomes our reference point, we use our wrath to separate ourselves from others with high walls topped with barbed wire and broken glass, rather than healthy boundaries which allow for intimacy. We believe that the best defense is a good offense and frequently attack other people before they have a chance to attack us, never stopping to consider that they may not have emotional assault on their agendas.

Take a look at the following words and circle the ones you'd use to most accurately describe yourself:

irritated	*scornful*	*resentful*	*serene*	*gentle*
indignant	*exasperated*	*bitter*	*calm*	*even-tempered*
burned up	*furious*	*impatient*	*pleasant*	*easygoing*
wrathful	*enraged*	*forgiving*	*tranquil*	*patient*

Now see if you notice a pattern. If your descriptors are heavily weighted on the left side of the page, you are carrying an excess of anger in your life. If every one of your descriptors is on the right side of the page, there's a good possibility that you're either denying the anger that you feel or that you believe under no circumstances should you feel outraged about anything.

On a sheet of paper, pretend you are dialoguing with your anger or your inability to recognize and feel anger. Ask it why it is a part of you. Give your anger or lack of it a voice and let it have its say about why it chooses to hurt you and how it can help you. Is it protecting you against something? If so, what? How does it most often manifest itself? By lashing out at others with words? By choking your expression with a viselike grip? Through silent sulks? Through stomachaches? Now ask your anger what it needs you to do in your physical life to allow it to relinquish control of you. If you have trouble feeling any anger at all, ask your anger to show itself to you. As you conclude writing, reassure your anger that you do not want it to go away entirely, that you want it to be a part of you when the situation is appropriate.

Fear/Courage

Now it is time to look at your fear or anxiety. As with anger, fear is not a bad emotion. It can be extremely useful in situations of danger. Our fear is often motivated from survival instincts. When we are threatened, fear signals us to run, to hide or to freeze like a startled deer until the danger passes.

When fear rules our lives and our thought processes on a full-time basis, the objects of that terror may not be dangerous at all. We automatically skitter away at even the slightest hint of risk and so, in addition to avoiding very real dangers, we run from growth and change. We tend to structure our lives in order never to confront our panic of the unknown and avoid having new experiences, feeling new emotions, meeting new people. Some of us get to the point where we fear ourselves, including our bodies, our thoughts, and our behavior. Our initial fears feed other fears until we are terrified to get a job, drive a car or leave the house.

The longer we fear, the more rigid we become, because we have to constrain our lives in tighter and tighter circles in order to avoid encountering perceived threats. We may learn to live by a magical system of rituals. If we always do our laundry on Sunday night and then one Sunday are prevented from doing it, we feel anxious and off-balanced — as if keeping to our schedule or doing everything on our list is the only way we have to prevent ourselves from slipping off the edge of the universe.

Often our fears are so deep and frightening, we are unable to give name to them. We may develop what mental health experts call *free-floating anxiety*, a low grade but constant feeling of impending disaster. Fear can cause us to be hypervigilant, always aware of what others around us are doing and saying. We might be easily startled and have difficulty concentrating. When fear becomes a constant companion, it ceases to be helpful to us and, instead, becomes harmful. We develop headaches and ulcers, high blood pressure and muscle tension.

Read the following adjectives and, again, circle the ones that accurately describe you now:

panicky	apprehensive	timid	uneasy	resolute
anxious	dreading	nervous	bold	rash
wary	cowardly	brave	courageous	reckless
insecure	confident	fearless	daring	foolhardy

Look at the answers you circled and see if they form a pattern. If you feel frightened or anxious most of the time, you may be paralyzed into inaction by what you see as threatening. If you are rash and reckless most of the time, then your fear blockage is preventing you from seeing ahead to the consequences of your actions. You tend to make a number of decisions you later regret. Often when we're acting with bravado, we aren't feeling courageous at all. Instead, we're wearing our recklessness like a mask to hide our inner anxiety.

Take another piece of paper and head it *FEAR*. Allow yourself to brainstorm, writing down all the things you know you're afraid of and all the things you think you might be afraid of if you allowed yourself to face the emotion of fear. Because you're writing everything without censoring yourself, your list may contain fears all the way from abandonment and AIDS to spiders and heights.

Fears are like allergies. They are usually rooted in a traumatic, sensitizing experience. Now do some detective work and make a note after each item on your list of when that particular fear came into being and the circumstances of its birth in your life. After you've done that, place a star by each fear on your list which serves a valid, protective purpose in your life today. Cross out the ones which you currently carry as useless baggage.

Now rank the things which frighten you from least to most potent. After you're done, jot down the uncomfortable physical feelings which accompany each fear. Not all of our fear triggers the same reactions. You might find your chest tightens and your breathing becomes restricted when you think of being left alone, but that your heart beats faster and your palms perspire when you see a spider. Listing the physical symptoms which accompany each of our fears, enables us to recognize better the source of those fears when they arise.

Look over your list and make a commitment to yourself to live the next few days in a state of mindfulness. Your job isn't to root out your fears and eradicate them, but to acknowledge them the moment you feel them. Whenever you notice physical symptoms of anxiety, tell yourself it's okay to be frightened. Ask yourself what you are afraid of in the current environment, then try tracing the fear back to its source.

Sadness/Joy

Sadness colors our lives so that our days seem to drag by as dull drab grey. Sometimes our pain can be profound and dramatic. At other times it is an all-pervasive blanket which covers our attitudes and dims our ability to perceive the world around us.

The emotion of sadness is a natural and normal reaction to grief. We feel grief not only when a loved one dies, but whenever we experience a loss. The grieving process kicks into operation when we remember the loss of child-hood from a parent's abuse, when we give up an old habit like smoking or eating sugar, and when we decide to rid ourselves of unhealthy patterns of relating to others. We may grieve over the pieces of our self-esteem we've sac-rificed in psychologically abusive relationships or about the times when our needs weren't met. When grief is prolonged and becomes depression, we need to seek pro-fessional help in order to move through to the other side of the dark cloud.

Read over the following adjectives and circle the ones which best apply to you:

despairing	*dejected*	*abandoned*	*happy*	*optimistic*
helpless	*unhappy*	*inconsolable*	*glad*	*joyful*
discouraged	*pained*	*despondent*	*cheerful*	*manic*
broken-hearted	*depressed*	*self-assured*	*sprightly*	*ecstatic*

If your circled words fell mainly on the left side of the page, you tend to view the world through murky glasses. Chances are some of your sadness has legitimate roots, but some of it may be self-pity. If you circled only the happy words on the right, you could be running from pain — the life of the party, a laugh-a-minute comedienne or a perpetual Pollyanna.

Once more take a piece of paper, but this time draw a picture of your sadness. What shape does it have? What color? What texture? What size? Now try writing the words for what you are sad about, either inside your drawing or tied to it with strings. Look at your picture for a minute then revise it or add more words if you need to.

Imagine you can hold your sadness in your hand. How does it feel? Heavy or light? Soft or hard? Wet or dry? Rough or smooth? How do *you* feel when you imagine you hold your sadness in your hand in front of you? If you gave your sadness a name, what would it be?

Address your sadness with the name you've given it and let it know that you acknowledge its presence, that you know it came into your life for a reason. Ask it when it came into your life. What purpose does it serve? What does it need from you in order to relinquish control over your thoughts and actions? At this point you might want to take a new piece of paper and have your sadness write a letter of reply to you, answering your questions.

If you feel silly doing these exercises, think for a time on why you feel silly and list the reasons. Perhaps you are still trying to deny your sadness. If you suspect this is the case, write down the worst things that could happen if you allowed yourself to feel emotional pain. When we give voice to our feelings, they can tell us amazing and insightful information. The self-knowledge they impart points the way toward inner healing.

Guilt And Shame/Self-Worth

Guilt is feeling remorse about things we've done, shame is remorse for who we are, regret for taking up space on the planet. Both excessive guilt and shame leave little room inside of us for a healthy self-concept to evolve.

Small doses of guilt are quite typical because guilt is the prod of the conscience. If we hadn't internalized some guilt from our parents' discipline as children, we might not be ethical people today. When we do something wrong, most of us feel uncomfortable. Often the anticipated discomfort of guilt is a deterrent which keeps us from hurting others. If we feel guilty after we've done something wrong, it spurs us to apologize.

When our parents gave us too many scoldings, we may as adults carry too much guilt for our own good. As we became involved in abusive relationships, the scoldings continued. Nothing we did stopped them. Nothing we did seemed to be right. In time an internal part of us took on the role of parent or verbally abusive partner and scolded ourselves for both real and imaginary infractions. It is when we carry huge overloaded gunny sacks of guilt around with us that we are in emotional trouble because our guilt solidifies into shame.

Shame causes us to reject ourselves and hate basic parts of us that we cannot change. We view ourselves as burdens rather than contributors. When we feel deep shame, we may try to escape it by using mood-altering substances. Chances are that a woman with an eating disorder, a drinking problem, a reliance on drugs, is running from her feelings of unworthiness.

Look at the words below and, once more, circle the ones you feel best describe how you feel right now:

humiliated	dishonored	valued	esteemed	vain
guilty	belittled	self-respecting	confident	grandiose
condemned	embarrassed	worthy	haughty	arrogant
ashamed	disgraced	self-assured	proud	entitled

If the adjectives on the left side of the page were the ones to receive the most circles, you're entangled in a guilt and shame trap and have an unrealistically low image of your self-worth and your potentials. Choosing descriptors on the right side of the page indicates that you have developed blind spots to your own flaws. We all have them — both the blind spots and the flaws. Wearing a permanent set of blinders to our imperfections and the possibility that we can and do make mistakes, leads to an artificially inflated picture of who we are. We may develop the belief that the world owes us a living, that everyone we meet owes us love and attention. Such feelings of entitlement and overbearing pride are often a cover for low self-esteem. Because we're so afraid that others will look inside us and be totally disgusted by our true selves, we hide behind a mask of grandiosity.

Give yourself a few minutes to make a list of everything you can think about, past and present, that you feel guilty or ashamed of. When you've finished, read over your list. If you've written details about something you've *done* which you feel uncomfortable with, then write "guilt" after it. If an item speaks to your essence, who you are, then write "shame" after it. If you had an affair and felt bad about it, deciding not to do it again, you experienced guilt. If you were sexually abused as a child and came to feel intensely uncomfortable with your sexuality, an undeniable part of your being, then you feel shame.

Initially it can be difficult to discriminate between feelings of guilt and feelings of shame, but making the determination is critical to recovery.

In Step Five we will work with our guilt, our remorse over our past actions, to alleviate it. We still need to be aware, however, that our underlying shame can linger long after we've dealt with our guilt. Our apologetic attitude for being alive, for taking up space and for breathing, has more than likely grown from things which were done to us, rather than things we did. We cannot take away abuses that happened in the past, but we can recognize their impact on our emotions and can change our attitudes about the past.

Go over your list one more time, paying special attention to the items you've labeled shame. Take a moment or two to think about each one and see if you can remember the event which initially triggered your feeling of shame. Perhaps a parent told you your birth was a mistake or emotionally abandoned you. Maybe you had difficulty having an orgasm and a partner said you were frigid or asexual. Write the event after each shame item.

Much of the criticism we receive has more to do with the person giving it than with us. Shame comes from blame. A parent who lacks parenting skills or a capacity to give love, blames a child and passes his or her shame along to that child. A man who feels sexually inadequate pins his discomfort with his sexuality on his partner to escape his own feelings of shame. When people tell us we're no good or we'll never change, chances are high it is themselves they are really talking about. With this in mind, check over your list again and mentally give up title to the shame you no longer want to own, relinquishing it to its original owner. The more shame we disown, the more space we have inside for self-esteem.

To end the exercise, on another piece of paper start making an inventory of all the things about yourself you like. These can be qualities you possess, skills or potentials. Include events, things and people in your life you're pleased with. Remember to write down your successes, no matter how small you believe them to be. In the beginning your list may not be very long, so write big and give yourself time. You might want to leave your list in a prominent place where you can add to it when you discover or remember a new strength.

Other emotional extremes you may wish to examine within yourself are:

Suspicion/Trust	*Satisfaction/Discontent*
Loneliness/Community	*Hate/Love*
Clarity/Confusion	*Boredom/Involvement*

Because we are unique individuals with our own personalities, each of us has an optimal configuration of
emotions, just as we have slightly different nutritional
requirements from others. Trying to impose a uniform
set of standards on the balance of our feelings might
make it faster for us to determine how we measure up,
but it is a shortcut with failings. Only by getting in touch
and in tune with our emotions, by knowing what we feel
and owning those feelings, can we gain an internal sense
of when we are emotionally balanced or off balance.
When we pay attention to our internal gyroscopes, we
are able more easily to keep our lives on course.

> *I am seeking to mindfully acknowledge and observe
> my emotions, to listen to what they have to say to me
> and to make friends with them as they lead me to a
> deeper understanding of myself.*

7

Step Four — Part II

We made a searching and fearless moral
inventory of ourselves.

*"Is it age or was it my nature to take
a bad time, block out the good times, until
any success became an accident and
failure seemed the only truth?"*

Lillian Hellman

When we allow our worldview to be colored by an excess of any emotion, be it euphoria or depression, anger or fear, shame or vanity, we attend to only that which contributes to our predominant emotion. If we get up on the wrong side of the bed, we'll be irritated by circumstances and remarks we'd not otherwise notice were we in a good mood. The days and months we feel the saddest seem to generate an unlimited number of occasions for failure. We lose objectivity along with our emotional balance.

An emotion held over a long period of time tends to crystallize into a belief about the universe and how it works. When our emotions rule, they limit our thinking capacity so that our most cherished beliefs may have little to do with reality. Instead they become rigid defenses, defenses which we must acknowledge if we are to grow.

Our distorted thinking takes many forms. We may come to believe that qualities are distributed on an all-or-nothing basis. Life is wonderful or it is awful. We are superb human beings or we are wretches. If people don't love us, they must hate us. If we aren't complete successes, then we must be total failures.

Perfectionistic thinking flows from this black/white polarization of our interior and exterior worlds. We view ourselves hyper-critically and stop taking risks in order to save ourself from potential failures. We put off doing things because we know that without practice we can't do them well. If we confessed we needed practice, then we'd be admitting we aren't already perfect. To admit that, causes us to fear that the world would crash down around our ears at best. At worst we would cease to exist. If we can't do something well, we don't do it. If we can't say anything right, we don't say it. Our lives become constrained to the point of self-suffocation.

When we cling too tightly to pain and do not express and allow our anger at that pain to dissipate, we minimize the positive feelings we have and the positive events around us by becoming pessimists. We brood over the worst and invariably expect it will happen. For us, every cloud has a black and gloomy lining. If another person makes friendly overtures, we immediately question their motives. We're reluctant to accept compliments or presents because we're sure they have strings attached. Since we dwell on the negative so constantly, we seem to attract negative people and events into our lives. Often our worst predictions *do* come true because we subconsciously set their wheels in motion.

In order to avoid further pain, we minimize and deny anything we perceive to be threatening to our current self-image, whether it is a smile and a cheery hello from a co-worker or a long-term, intensely abusive relationship. At the same time we magnify our relatively nonthreatening troubles to draw our attention away from the real source of our discomfort. A normally minor hassle, like losing a button or getting a flat tire, becomes an enormous stumbling block as we obsess for days over it. The phrase, "Making mountains out of molehills" appears to be invented expressly for us.

Projection

Because we find it difficult to come to terms with ourselves and be honest about the feelings which have us by the throat, we may project our own emotions onto others. Instead of admitting that we've had a bad day and are grouchy and overly sensitive, we turn our antennae outward.

"The people around me sure are grouchy today," we think. "All they seem to want to do is pick a fight."

Sometimes we project our own character flaws onto others so that we do not have to admit them within ourselves. When Jesus talked about removing the beam from our own eye before we try to pick out a splinter from our neighbor's, he was talking about projecting our shortcomings onto others. Our fear of self-confrontation tends to take shape in beliefs about other people. People rarely tell the truth, we think. People are always out for what they can get. If a person has a chance to stab you in the back, he'll do it.

Rationalization

The logical second stage of projection is rationalization. We use the imagined laws which we believe govern other peoples' behavior to justify our own. When you believe other people are out to get you, you can justify acting out your anger without ever taking the responsibility for the feeling or action by telling yourself you'd better get them first. If other people rarely tell the truth, then why should you? If people are out for all they can get, you'd darned well better grab your share first. The times we *aren't*

defensively selfish or untruthful or hurtful, we feel inor-
dinately self-righteous.

When we don't use rationalization as an excuse to avoid
owning our emotions and behavior, we may distort our
thinking so that we see cause and effect where none
exists. Other people make us feel things, say things or do
things, we wouldn't normally feel, say or do. This twisted
logic is a carry over from childhood when people bigger
than us, the people who dished out the food and provided
shelter from the elements, could force us to do things we
didn't want to do. As adults, however, we can meet our
basic survival needs. If we feel, do or say things other
people want us to, we act out of choice. As adults, people-
pleasing isn't a matter of life or death as it was for us as
children. If we look at our lives objectively, rarely do our
partners or children or parents or friends or even society
as a whole, force us to act against our wills. They may
give us some unpleasant consequences for going against
their wishes, but they aren't holding a gun to our heads.

Those of us who sidestep responsibility for emotions
and behavior as a defense, don't do so for free. We often
extract a price in the form of entitlement, a hidden agenda
in our relationships. We give and give, and all the time we
are secretly adding up the debts that others or life itself
owes us. When the debts mount up to a sufficiently high
level to spur us to assertiveness, we collect by strong-
arming with guilt those we feel are obligated to us. "After
all I've done for you . . ." becomes our motto.

These emotional defense systems limit our options for
problem-solving and cramp our enjoyment of life. As long
as we continue to allow our emotions to dominate us and
as long as we limit our palette of feelings to one or two
which dominate our lives, we are unable to respond to
situations by choosing from the entire spectrum of emotions. It is no wonder we react inappropriately and un-
creatively to life more often than we wish.

When we take our mental inventory, we acknowledge
and examine the "laws to live by" which we inherited and

accepted unquestioningly from our families of origin and from our culture. We also need to discover and take a long hard look at those which were constructed as defense mechanisms to protect ourselves from emotional hurt.

Examining Family Rules

Every family has rules. Some go back generations. Dysfunctional families' rules tend to include: Don't feel; don't express feelings; don't trust and don't talk about family problems to strangers. Although the rules may not be stated so clearly, because in many families it's a rule not to talk about the rules, they tend to reveal themselves in favorite family sayings like, "Don't air your dirty laundry in public" or "Pride goeth before a fall."

Take some quiet time and list your family mottoes. You might start with your parents' favorite sayings and then write down your grandparents' tried and true homilies.

Next, add the cultural rules you've heard and assimilated without question. We learn cultural rules within our families and from teachers and friends, as well as from TV, radio, movies, magazines and books. Some we discard, but others we take on as truths. "Women shouldn't act too smart," "Older women naturally lose interest in sex," "Women need to protect the male ego and women are more emotional than men," are some examples of these cultural dictums.

Finally, write your own rules for living which you've collected from the school of hard knocks, both as a child and as an adult. Most of our personal rules are phrased with shoulds and oughts. "I shouldn't ever say no to sex." "I should always give in to my parents' wishes and demands." "I ought to always wear perfume and shave my legs every other day."

These behavior guidelines spring from our more general blanket attitudes toward life and its components. Our worldviews are usually worded in the form of flat statements. When we first develop an attitude toward life, we consciously repeat it to ourselves but in time there is no need to. We file away our personal "facts of life" in our subconscious, often acting on them without knowing they exist. As you begin writing, you can use some of the following starting points to help get your ideas flowing.

People are	Trust leads to . . . .
The world is	Emotions are . . . .
Love is	Punishment is . . . .
Men are	Honesty gets you . . . .

The best way to get ahead is . . . .
People like people who will . . . .

Now read over your lists and cross out the rules that at this point in your life you view as silly or outdated. As you reread the remaining items, rank them in their order of importance for survival in the world. After each rule, jot down the consequence you believe would happen to you if you broke it. For example if you didn't shave your legs regularly, men might find you disgusting. If you said no to sex, your partner might get angry and leave you for another woman. If people weren't motivated by greed, you might have to trust them and learn more generosity.

Examine the consequences for their current potency. Some, like fear of abandonment or being tricked by greedy people, may be very powerful, while others, such as having your parents get irritated with you, may hold little threat to you as an adult. When we look at the feared consequences we write down, we often see patterns or themes emerging. Simply knowing they're present provides us with a choice to respond or to detach from them and invent newer, more positive themes for our lives.

Examine each rule on your list carefully and determine if it is a product of all-or-nothing thinking, perfectionism, minimization or magnification, denial, projection, rationalization, entitlement or emotional reasoning. When you discover a law of life based on faulty reasoning, label it with the type of distorted thinking which spawned it.

An honest assessment of whether your rules for living are currently realistic and are helpful to you, rather than harmful, gives important clues to what works and what is just excess baggage. Scrutinizing the feared consequences of breaking the rules also hints at which are realistically threatening and which were scary at one point, but have currently lost their power over you. This knowledge is a useful tool to put us more in touch with ourselves. We can make decisions based on a clear perspective of our interior reality, rather than on some churning internal soup made from unknown emotional ingredients.

Body Inventory

In addition to looking at our mental smoke screens, we need to probe our physical state. Do we eat nutritious meals and make sure we get enough rest? Do we exercise and try to maintain our optimum weight? When we look at ourselves naked in a full-length mirror, do we like what we see? Many women don't — even beautiful ones.

At this point it might be a good idea to make yet another list, this time of things you like about your body, your physical good points. Then make a second list of the parts of your body you don't like. Go over each item and determine whether or not you can change it or will need to change your attitude toward it.

Often, when we're in emotional pain, we neglect our health because we have other things on our mind. The more we ignore our physical well-being, the worse we look and the worse our bodies feel. This, in turn, triggers another bout of self-loathing so we neglect our health and appearance even more. By giving ourselves and our life-styles close scrutiny, we can determine what we want to change, including what we eat, how much we sleep and how much stress we allow into our lives.

Since many of us have lost touch with our physical bodies, preferring to live in our heads, it may have been years since we listened with our inner ear to what our body is trying to tell us about our eating habits, our sleep and stress. We pay attention to our physical being only when our aches and pains become unbearable. We may let health problems go far too long before we seek medical treatment. If it has been years since you've had a physical, now is the time to get one.

Our well-being — physical, mental and emotional — can be affected by our relationships to substances as well as to people. Too often we learn as children to fill up an empty psychic space with cookies or snacks. We come to depend on food, a poor substitute, to give us emotional nurturing and support, in the meantime losing touch with our physical hunger. Or we may turn to alcohol or drugs in a way of self-medicating our emotional pain. We smoke too much or eat too much sugar to get us up for the day. We may take tranquilizers at night to put us under. All the time we distance ourselves further and further from what our bodies need and what our hearts are feeling.

This self-evaluation is a time to honestly and fearlessly confront our physical health and our relationship to substances so that we can begin healing our bodies, as well as our minds and spirits.

Too often our relationships to the other people in our lives, especially our partners, take on the characteristics of our connection to drugs or alcohol. We relate addictively, depending on someone or something outside of us to "fix" us and make us whole. The fact that it doesn't work, doesn't stop our craving. In fact we desperately crave more and more quick "fixes." The sicker our relationships become, the more firmly convinced we are that we cannot survive without them.

Many of us who are addicted to emotionally abusive relationships manage to maintain other relationships in our lives which are healthy — if we don't get too close to the friend in question or if the friend is a woman or if it's purely a work-related relationship or a relationship with a child. Others find addictive patterns have permeated the entirety of their association with other human beings.

Relationship Checklist

The final part of this chapter consists of a checklist of ways of relating to others. You are asked to respond with a "yes" or "no," depending on how you feel the statement applies to your feelings about and dealings with your partner. In addition, there's a second blank for a response for your feelings about and dealings with others. If you think it would be more useful to you if you used the second response to assess how you relate to someone specific like a parent, a close friend or your child or children, then, by all means, do so.

	With Partner	With Others
I take responsibility for my own feelings and thoughts.	_____	_____
I resist the temptation to "fix" others' emotional and physical needs.	_____	_____
I am able to delegate responsibility for chores without feeling guilt.	_____	_____
When I set a task for myself I usually complete it without procrastination.	_____	_____
I set aside time to relax and play.	_____	_____
When I feel overburdened, I solve the problem rather than gripe about it.	_____	_____
I am a capable and competent person.	_____	_____
I am willing to let others be the center of attention sometimes.	_____	_____
I feel confident and comfortable being who I am.	_____	_____
I am pleased with my physical body.	_____	_____
At times I enjoy being alone.	_____	_____

	With Partner	With Others
I feel it is okay for me to make mistakes.	_____	_____
I am tolerant when others make mistakes.	_____	_____
When I need help, I know where to get it and am not afraid to do so.	_____	_____
I am able to rely on myself to meet many of my emotional needs.	_____	_____
I continue to grow, learn and change.	_____	_____
I am able to allow others to grow, learn and change.	_____	_____
I can tolerate ambiguity.	_____	_____
My thoughts aren't often scattered.	_____	_____
Mostly my life and environment are in order.	_____	_____
I enjoy setting realistic goals.	_____	_____
Usually I know what I'm feeling.	_____	_____
I resist trying to read others' minds. I respect my feelings.	_____	_____
I respect the rights of others to feel as they do.	_____	_____
I remain in the present situation and seldom "tune out."	_____	_____
I work out my emotional states rather than act them out.	_____	_____
Although I listen to my emotions, I am rarely overcome by them.	_____	_____
After I've acknowledged my feelings, I'm ready to sit down and solve my problem.	_____	_____

	With Partner	With Others
I can rationally discuss my feelings.	___	___
I'm honest with myself.	___	___
I honestly represent myself to others.	___	___
I'm able to keep my opinion to myself when it would be inappropriate to express it.	___	___
I rarely tell others their flaws "for their own good."	___	___
When I criticize others, I do so constructively.	___	___
I can listen to criticism from others without attacking or feeling crushed.	___	___
When I make a mistake, I'm willing to admit it.	___	___
I'm able to laugh at life.	___	___
I'm able to laugh at myself when I'm acting ridiculous.	___	___
I appreciate others' sense of humor.	___	___
I believe that my needs can be met.	___	___
I express them assertively to increase their chances of being met.	___	___
I listen attentively to the needs, concerns and feelings of others.	___	___
I understand that they won't always be met immediately even by me.	___	___
I know that no one except me can ever fully understand me.	___	___
I have a right to my needs and wishes.	___	___

	With Partner	With Others
I do not expect others to "fix" me.	_____	_____
I am taking steps to make my life the way I want it to be.	_____	_____
I realize there are things in life I can't control.	_____	_____
I know I cannot control other people.	_____	_____
I don't feel superior to others.	_____	_____
I don't feel inferior to others.	_____	_____
I believe I am a unique and valuable person.	_____	_____
I am in charge of my fulfillment and happiness.	_____	_____
I have hobbies and friends outside the relationship.	_____	_____
I have other friends.	_____	_____
I don't lean on others or "smother" them.	_____	_____
I am able to share with others.	_____	_____
I prefer to act rather than to react to people and situations.	_____	_____
I analyze what people in power say rather than automatically complying.	_____	_____
I very rarely rebel just to get even or get back at another person.	_____	_____
If this relationship were to end, I could survive.	_____	_____
I like to do things for others.	_____	_____
I enjoy having people do nice things for me.	_____	_____

	With Partner	With Others
I don't buy people or relationships.	___	___
I don't let people buy my affection.	___	___
I am able to say no to people.	___	___
I am able to say yes to people.	___	___
I trust others who are worthy of my trust.	___	___
I am loyal, but can end relationships when they become destructive.	___	___
I am willing to risk being real.	___	___

While these statements don't cover every single aspect of our relationships with others, our responses give us a picture of our strengths and our weaknesses. Because co-addictive patterns of relating aren't limited to intimate couples only, we may find on examination that we've allowed ourselves to slip into an emotionally abusive relationship with a boss, with a parent or with a child.

When we examine our relationships, we may discover they work fine outside of our homes, but fall apart with our partners. In addition, some of our strong points may be so strong, they turn into negatives. For example, we may be so independent, we've become isolated or so organized and goal-oriented, we're rigid. We may be so expressive of our needs, we're demanding.

When you've finished looking at how you relate to your partner and others, read over the statements once more, this time seeing how they apply to your relationship to your Higher Power. Many times we find that our spiritual side is off kilter in the same areas as our other relationships. We may minimize our needs and never express them to our Higher Power, or we may go to the other extreme and present a list of demands for immediate gratification. We may see ourselves as worms in the eyes of the Cosmic Force or we may see ourselves as grandiose.

Our problems are often really imbalances, either having too much of a quality or not having developed enough
of it. We are precariously poised on the end of the teeter-
totter where our ups and downs are intense and frightening. The closer we get to the fulcrum, the more stable
our lives grow. When we inventory ourselves honestly,
we determine our lacks and excesses, so we can move
toward the equilibrium in our lives that we need to
become centered.

> *I honestly acknowledge and claim ownership of the*
> *qualities which make me a unique individual. I love*
> *and respect myself and affirm that I can change and*
> *grow into the person I want to become.*

8

Step Five

We admitted to God, to ourselves and to another
human being the exact nature of our wrongs.

*"As awareness increases, the need for personal
secrecy almost proportionally decreases."*

Charlotte Painter

So far our change and growth have been an individual
process conducted in the solitude of our own hearts and
minds. We have not needed other people to help us as we
progressed up to this point. In fact, the people around us
may not have known what we were up to unless we
chose to tell them. Step Five presents us with another
challenge, moving us out of our solitary circle of transformation, asking that we practice openness and honesty
first with our Higher Power and with ourselves, then
finally expanding that practice with another human being.

Step Five provides the spring thaw which melts the last
of our frozen crust of denial and allows the remaining,
stubborn blocks of solidified defense to dislodge and flow

down the stream so that our emotions may move through us unimpeded. Like melting ice, the process is a gradual one and structured so that we go from the easiest to the most difficult challenge in small manageable steps.

The dictionary defines "to admit" as "to concede as true." We are required to claim ownership of the inventory we made in Step Four, acknowledging that it is true and belongs to us as much as our arms or legs or ears or eyes. When we make this admission, we allow another type of admission, one the dictionary defines as "permitting entry." Once we proclaim the validity of who we are — the good parts and the bad — we move past our shame and gain access to ourselves. This begins a life-long interior exploration process. We are no longer compelled to flee from who we are or to live on the surface.

Because we've stopped running scared from who we are, we no longer have to block out intimacy in order to hide our true selves from others and maintain our own integrity. Neither do we need to allow others to run rampant over our interior landscape since in confessing and, thus accepting ourselves, we reclaim the power to permit or deny their access to our deepest selves. Whether we allow others inside or keep them at a distance becomes our choice rather than a compulsion.

When we are honest with our Higher Power, ourselves and another person about exactly who we are at this moment, we transcend the shame and self-loathing upon which so much of our lives has been founded. No longer is it necessary for us to suffer from spiritual, emotional and intellectual blockage in order to protect ourselves from rejection and the hurt rejection causes us. Certainly we will experience hurt, fear and anger, but because we've allowed the barriers inside ourselves to melt, those unpleasant feelings will flow through and out of us, rather than stagnating and poisoning our thoughts, feelings and relationships. In letting go of the last vestiges of denial, we open ourselves to become channels for the energy of the Higher Power to work in our lives.

Self-knowledge

If we are to effectively confess the exact nature of our wrongs, we must face the reality of who we are head-on and give up our old defenses against self-knowledge and self-acceptance. Often our fear of inner reality stops us at the Fifth Step. It is quite possible to make a searching and fearless Fourth Step moral inventory and then twist it to reinforce our comfortable old defense systems rather than dissolving them. When we do this, we tend to use the patterns of distorted thinking discussed earlier.

We might minimize our weaknesses, telling ourselves that they don't really matter — so why even bother to talk about them? We may maximize them until they over-whelm us and we believe that if we confessed them, we'd be admitting to being the most horrible person alive. Our all-or-nothing thinking may convince us that we're either a bundle of flaws or we're perfect. There's no middle ground, so we restructure our inventory to fit into a mutually exclusive dualistic paradigm.

Even when we don't stumble over these obstacles to full and open admission, we may get caught up in rationalizing our defects and lack of balance, telling ourselves that we can't help being the way we are because of our nasty childhoods or because we were born with a certain per-sonality, that our defects are genetic. Although past expe-riences and heredity are undoubtedly factors which shape us, if we get too caught up in analyzing why we are, we may lose sight of who we are. Instead of an admission, we construct a detailed case study, devoting our energy to psychoanalyzing ourselves so that we don't have to own up to or accept our essence — we're too busy explaining it to acknowledge it.

Another way we may sabotage Step Five is to use it as a gripe session to ventilate our emotions and to blame other people for what we don't like about ourselves. When we blame, we shift responsibility for ourselves onto others and if totally caught up in finger pointing, we may manage to completely disown our negative qualities, shifting title to our parents or partner. Instead of working on ourselves, we hook back into the old cycle of giving others power over us and desperately trying to control them so that our lives will be manageable.

If as you work Step Five you find yourself using distorted thinking, rationalization or blaming in order to distance yourself from confronting and confessing who you are, you need to make a judicious retreat and rework the first Four Steps until you are ready to move ahead. It takes courage to openly confess our defects. That foundation of courage is built on admitting our powerlessness, our belief in a Higher Power, turning our lives over to that Power and upon discovering ourselves.

Confession To Our Higher Power

Once we've inventoried ourselves, our first task is to admit to God/dess the exact nature of our wrongs. Because our Higher Power is all-knowing, to be less than honest or to gloss over our defects in an attempt to be self-servingly vague is a futile exercise. Since the Higher Power already knows everything about us, it may seem redundant to spell everything out, but the act of admitting or confessing, is essential to the healing process. It is up to us to diagnose ourselves and to share that information with the Higher Power, making the first move toward initiating an honest relationship with God/dess.

When we confess, we clean out our wounds. The process of owning our defects and acknowledging that we are aware they are wrongs, gets them out in the open and begins dissipating our guilt over them. Guilt over things we've said or done which have hurt ourselves or others, grows like an infection in the darkness and secrecy of denial. When we face reality, we peel off our dirty tattered bandages to let the sunlight and air in, disinfecting our souls.

Admitting our wrongs to ourselves is simply a continuation of Step Four, accepting ourselves as we are with all levels of our being, not just our intellects. Only when we can admit our wrongs with our hearts and spirits, as well as our minds, can we hope to relate to others with authenticity. Until we accept ourselves we must constantly project false images on our exterior surfaces, hoping to fool others into thinking we are different than we really are. Although we may not con others from a malicious desire to trick them, we do indeed deceive. Pulling the plug on our self-deception stops the projector from running. When we no longer delude ourselves, we cease to play out illusions for others.

Admitting Our Wrongs To Another

The third part of Step Five, admitting our wrongs to another human being, is often the most difficult part of the step for us. Because so many of us grew up in homes where there was little acceptance and honest communication, we often have an extremely difficult time relating to others. In fact, our emotionally and verbally abusive marriages may have saved us from ever having to take the risk of openness and honesty, a risk our past had not prepared us to take.

Women who experienced difficult childhoods and/or abusive marriages tend to be hypervigilant, always trying to pick up signals to gauge how others are reacting to them and thinking about them, so that they can change what they're trying to say and how they're saying it. When you lived with a partner who blew up at the slightest provocation, you learned to detect the most subtle signals of his discomfort. Chances are you censored what you had to say, sugar-coating it or turning it inside out. In the Fifth Step, telling the truth about ourselves is crucial, no matter how our listener reacts. If we distort the content of what we're saying, we are denying our inner reality and sabotaging our recovery.

Don't Tell . . .

It becomes very important, then, to exercise caution in selecting a person to hear your Fifth Step, someone who will patiently listen in a nonjudgmental manner. Although your partner may be the one person currently in your life

who knows you best, he is *not* the one to listen to you
admit your wrongs. That would be the same as a recovering alcoholic requesting an old and unreformed drinking
buddy to hear her admission. It is also not a good idea to
do your Fifth Step with a woman friend also involved in
a psychologically abusive relationship. Someone still enmeshed in the emotional and verbal abuse cycle, will be so
locked in denial, they cannot listen to what you have to
say without judgment.

By the same token, some people have an intense need to
rescue others and problem solve for them. If you choose
such a person for your Fifth Step partner, you run the
risk of being told how to "save" your relationship and
yourself. You do not need advice. You need someone who
will listen and encourage you to talk without jumping in
and taking responsibility for curing what ails you.

You may find that other friends and acquaintances are
amateur analysts who take great delight in guessing the
hidden motivations of the people they encounter. These
folks often use psychological jargon to label you. "You're
a passive/aggressive with masochistic tendencies. You
must really hate your mother," you might hear one of
them say. Although analyzing what makes people tick can
be a fascinating avocation, one we all indulge in from time
to time, the Fifth Step is not a therapy session. In order
for it to work, your co-stepper needs only to listen, not to
figure you out and report their findings back to you.

Neither is the Fifth Step the time or place for a pep rally.
While it's very encouraging and empowering to know you
have a cheering section behind you as you work to transcend an emotionally abusive relationship, admitting your
flaws to a listener who will commiserate with you over
what a nasty bum your partner is or who will encourage
you to show him a thing or two, does you no good in the
long run. Even though you may get a temporary boost
from the understanding or pity such a person can provide,
in the long run you'll move further from taking complete
responsibility for who you are and fall into the trap of

blame and self-pity. It is important to realize that although the vociferous cheerleaders are well-meaning, more often than not they're projecting their own needs onto you so that *you* can act them out.

Where Do You Find A Listener?

Where do you go to find a person who will be willing to listen as you admit your shortcomings? Finding a willing helper can be difficult since most of us who have been in emotionally abusive relationships for any length of time are isolated, having cut off contact with friends. Probably the most fruitful place to search for someone to listen to your Fifth Step is at a Twelve-Step group. If there are none which deal specifically with emotionally abusive relationships in your area, such as Co-dependents Anonymous, you may be able to begin by attending a group for adult children of alcoholics or dysfunctional families.

A therapist who is familiar with the problems of victims of emotional abuse can be another resource. If you choose to go this route, be sure you make it clear at the outset what you want to do, so that even if you're involved in therapy, you can set aside a session or two to focus solely on Fifth-Step work.

Finally, this step may provide motivation to make friendships with women you like and trust as you seek out one of them to hear your admission. One of the most healing things we can do during the recovery process is to surround ourselves with support networks — in essence, families of choice who accept us as we are, treat us with dignity and respect and who help us to learn to form healthy relationships. Within these networks we can experiment with having fun, giving and receiving affection and attention and with finding the level of healthy interdependence which is most comfortable for us.

Our Difficulty In Reaching Out

Because so many of us grew up in isolation and found emotionally abusive relationships, where we were in solitary confinement as adults, we may stop ourselves from reaching out. We still feel awkward or foolish when we attempt to make friends, even when we're sure our Higher Power hasn't rejected us and we've made great strides toward self-acceptance. From our parents and later, from our husbands, we acquired a number of beliefs which were necessary to keep us isolated and the dysfunctional relationship viable. Making connections with people outside our primary relationships is a powerful antidote to emotional abuse. If it weren't, abusers wouldn't instinctively insist on a closed family system as their most powerful weapon to control us. We can gain the courage to break out of our solitude by examining some of the isolationist beliefs we carry and evaluating their relevance to our lives today.

Certainly most of us who grew up in dysfunctional families learned early on not to talk about what we thought and how we felt. We were schooled not to reveal ourselves to family members or people outside of our families. When our words or actions or even our facial expressions and posture revealed to the world that our family of origin was less than perfect, we were punished and love and approval were withheld from us for our disloyalty. How dare we be anything but happy?

When we carry this don't-air-your-dirty-laundry-in-public rule into adult life, we may feel that to discuss anything but superficial matters is a betrayal of our partner. We let the no-talk rule keep us from therapy, from finding support groups and from forming all but the most casual friendships. When we do talk to people, we cover our feelings with masks of pseudo-happiness so they will not discover our pain and realize that our relationship with our partner is anything but blissful.

The Don't-Trust Rule

Often a blanket untrustworthiness of other human beings is the reason our parents gave us (and our partner gives us today) for holding ourselves apart from others. We may have internalized the fear that to form friendships and to reveal our true selves invites others to tell our secrets or figuratively stab us in the back by betraying our confidence.

In addition we've learned from the actions of parents and partners that people generally break their promises and their word is not to be trusted. Since we may not feel worthy of being treated well, we tend to look at the kindnesses of others as manipulative ploys. They must want something from us. Otherwise why would they bother to even notice we're alive?

Our low self-concept and fear of betrayal serve as magnets to attract just the type of people we're most afraid of attracting to us. We may turn a blind eye to potential friends who are kind, generous and honest people because they either bore us or cause us to feel discomfort — we simply don't know how to act around them. If, when we take the risk of reaching outside of ourselves to make friends, we get burned by our unwise choices, that serves to reinforce our belief that to be befriended and to allow ourselves vulnerability invariably brings negative consequences. Rarely do we understand that we've had a hand in making our pessimistic predictions become reality.

Our fear of abandonment can cause some real barriers to relating to others, too. As children, our very survival depended upon the caretaking of our parents. When we sensed they were intensely displeased with us to the point of not loving us, we learned to put on an act, to insure their continuing presence in our lives. When we formed relationships with men, we continued this tactic, firmly believing that if anyone *really* knew us, they wouldn't like us and would leave us.

Releasing Our Fears To Reach Out

Many times as adults we may tell ourselves that other people don't want to listen to us, that to ask another to do anything, even hear our Fifth Step, is a major imposition. At times we *may* lean too heavily on others, needing constant reassurance, then becoming phobic of even balanced interdependence. Beneath all of our excuses for avoiding friendship lies our terror of abandonment. We push people away from us before they have a chance to hurt us by dumping us, forgetting that as adults whether or not an individual chooses to remain a friend to us is not a life or death matter.

The Fifth Step demands that we release our fears of revealing ourselves to others, of trusting people then being abandoned. If we do it sincerely, our admission of our wrongs to our Higher Power, to ourselves and to another human being, cannot be a con job or an act. We need to reach out in good faith and draw others to us who will listen to our honest inventory and who will accept us for what we are — human beings in a process of healing, growth and change.

> *I am absolutely honest in my dealings with my Higher Power, myself and with others. I am reaching out, learning to trust and finding enjoyment in being a member of the human family.*

9

Step Six

**We were entirely ready to have our Higher Power
remove all these defects of character.**

*"We build up defenses slowly,
brick by brick, cementing them with our
fear and anguish; and then, when they are no
longer needed, we cannot bear to tear them down.
We have leaned on them too long. Our lives
have been shaped to fit them, emotions have
learned to flow under them, our vocabulary has
entwined itself around them until they
are almost hidden from us."*

Lillian Smith

Before we can let go of them, we must assess our attachment to each of our shortcomings as honestly as we assessed the shortcomings themselves. Some of us are more willing to let go of our defenses and maladaptive ways of coping than others are. We are ready to release some shortcomings faster than others. Working the Sixth

Step requires taking the time we need to see how attached we are to each of our defense mechanisms and imbalances, evaluating the possible consequences of change in our lives, then setting up the mental conditions so that we can feel completely ready to wave goodbye to our old habits. It's a process which doesn't happen overnight.

How many times have we told ourselves, "I'd give any-thing to be different from the way I am now?" We buy self-help books, take effectiveness seminars and tune in to problem-oriented talk shows on TV. We go on diets and carefully study the make-over articles in women's maga-zines. We have our colors analyzed or our auras read. Un-fortunately, despite what we may tell ourselves and others, we still cling desperately to our inadequacies and excesses, no matter how much trouble they cause. The truth of the matter is that we know all too well how to function as a fat person, a flighty person, a nervous wreck or a victim but have no idea whatsoever how to cope as a slender, focused or serene heroine. Our fear of the unknown can be overwhelming when we contemplate changing.

We may crave honest and loving relationships, but if we're truthful with ourselves, we must admit we've run from them or found a way to shape them into the old familiar emotionally abusive pattern. We convince our-selves that men who treat us with consistent affection and respect are boring or that there's something wrong with them for loving us. They must be wimps.

Some of us feel more anxious when our love relationships are going smoothly than when they are crumbling down around our ears. Because so many of our coping strategies are designed to deal with life's rough places, we are discon-certed during the smooth spots when there's little or noth-ing for us to do and we're simply required to *be*.

Habits are difficult to break, especially old feeling, thought and action patterns which have been deeply etched in our physical and emotional circuit boards. Our thoughts, feelings and actions are literally stuck in a rut. The Sixth Step doesn't ask us to break out of the familiar mold by ourselves. Our Higher Power is in charge of that. It only requires that we are entirely ready to have our defects removed. Although willingness may be easy to attain on an intellectual level, our emotional selves usually aren't so eager for the transformation to take place, so we become our own worst enemy and sabotage our Higher Power's efforts. In order for any lasting transition to occur all the parts of our being — rational, emotional, physical and spiritual — must be aligned and completely ready for the process to happen.

Fear is the major stumbling block to this alignment. Some of us are afraid we might not be able to change, that we'll fail miserably and be proven weak or lacking in will. Others fear success because to triumph over defects would mean that we were different than we believed. The dissonance is anxiety provoking.

Because we know that our changing will have consequences, not only for us but for those around us, we may be frightened that our transformation will result in being unloved and abandoned. We jealously guard the investment of time and energy we've made in our relationships up to this point and resist doing anything that will put them at risk. In order to protect ourselves from risking the unknown, we hang onto the tattered baggage of habit, even though we know it weighs us down and guarantees failure. We are wary of giving up our habits because they have served us well.

When we fight against the removal of our character defects, we are attempting to control the pain we feel when things don't happen to work out the way we want them to. If we set out knowing we'll fail, and we do eventually fail, we're in charge of the timing and degree of our failure, so it comes as no surprise. We experience the dull ache of, "Oh well, I never could do anything right," rather than a sharp emotional stab of disappointment.

In the past we may have been rewarded for failing. When we fell down, people gave us sympathy or pity. Sometimes they rushed in to rescue us, to fix our lives and make them okay again, as we have tried to do with our partners. Our saviors would work to solve our problems, taking responsibility for both the problem and the solution, letting us off the hook. If we failed again, it would be their fault, not ours. After all we were only following directions. If when we were children, we received attention only for exhibiting incompetence or making messes of our lives, we may have come to believe that only when we're feeling awful and acting in self-defeating ways will people love us. We forget that pity and rescuing aren't necessarily signs of love.

Some of us were raised in families who lived by mottoes like, "Don't get your hopes up," or, "If you want anything too badly, you'll end up disappointed." Instead of practicing positive thinking, our parents may have filled their homes and our lives with negativistic imagery — behind every dark cloud, there's another dark cloud. If we were exposed to this thinking, we quickly discovered we'd be ridiculed or scolded "for our own good" if we were self-affirming and trusting. Instead we learned to be self-denying and suspicious of what life might have to offer. It only made sense. After all, much of what went on inside our families was negative. We became experts at predicting the worst that could possibly happen if we did anything new and consequently many of us don't expose ourselves to new experiences today. We internalized the doomsaying and now ridicule ourselves when we even toy with the idea of taking a class, going on a diet or forming a new friendship, stopping ourselves before we start.

We have found failure to be more comfortable than success because succeeding doesn't fit in with our self-image. That picture of ourselves is a collage of bits and pieces provided by our family of origin, our significant others and our own experiences in the world. We may believe without question that women ought to make less money than men or ought to defer their needs to serve the men they love. We may feel that mothers should never be angry with their children, that we, like children, ought to be seen but not heard. We may think we aren't capable of ever doing anything right or that we're not very bright or that we're responsible for the feelings of others.

Releasing Our Self-Limitations

It takes time to give up this self-limiting set of beliefs. Each piece needs to be peeled away layer by layer before we are willing to have our shortcomings removed. When our image of ourselves is colored with self-loathing and defeatism, the prospect of being a happy, fulfilled and fully functioning individual can be scary. There's too big a gap between what we perceive as the real us and what we perceive as beyond our reach.

We can work for change by re-examining the limiting worldviews we wrote down when we did Step Four and by transforming them into positive ones, substituting "can" and "will" for "can't" and "should." Using this technique, "I can't ever do anything right" becomes, "I can do many things and do them well." By writing these affirmations down and regularly repeating them to ourselves, we internalize them and soon can act as if they were true, slowly growing accustomed to the notion that we are capable of change. We harness the power of self-fulfilling prophesy and use it to prepare ourselves for positive experiences to enter our lives, rather than setting up conditions for the negative to occur.

Since our energy has been so wrapped up in relationships, we fear the impact our changing will have on our ties with our partner. Sometimes when we stop focusing on reforming the man we love and center instead on releasing our shortcomings, the relationships improve. Our willingness to let go of our defenses and defects creates a vacuum for our Higher Power to fill with openness and strength. In the process our partner is subtly pushed into changing in positive directions because we no longer collude in playing the psychological abuse game. Our transformation starts to transform him.

Relationships

Some women choose as they work Step Six to remain
in the relationship even though their partner stubbornly
clings to his old ways of relating. Because they've pulled
their focus back from the man in their life, and are no
longer expending futile energy on trying to control and
change him, they are able to achieve serenity and inner
fulfillment. They can tolerate his outbursts without taking responsibility for them or letting his rage affect their
self-concept or the way they live their lives. They no
longer delude themselves into thinking they are forced
into remaining in the relationship, but can see it as an
option they have chosen.

Other women decide to terminate their relationships
with men who continue to verbally and psychologically
abuse them because they no longer can tolerate that life-
style. This decision isn't an easy one to make, but sometimes it is a necessary one, especially when the verbal
abuse increases over an extended period of time.

It is possible that your partner may be so triggered by
the changes he sees in you, he begins threatening physical
violence or actively carrying it out in an attempt to control you and the relationship. Even if you sense that this
may be a short-term reaction, a last-ditch effort to play
by the old rules, your physical safety must come first.
Allowing yourself to be hit, pushed, slapped or worse is
destructive to you and to the man in your life. If physical
violence occurs, remove yourself from the scene and
seek professional help.

Some women remain committed to the viability of the
relationship, but their partners feel the marriage has
reached the point of no return, that there is either no way
to make it better or that they do not wish to change it.

When our partners decide to leave, we must face the
pain of rejection and abandonment. Since we've structured our lives to avoid being abandoned, this is a time
when it is tempting to give up on our healing and regress
in an attempt to win a man back. It becomes inviting to

control and manipulate him into staying with us, wounding ourselves in the process. When we do this, we have no one to blame but ourselves for the unhappy circumstances of our lives. Clinging to another person who would rather not be with us is both unsatisfying and anxiety-provoking. Nonetheless, if we are terrified at the possibility of having to make it through life on our own, the relationship's end may be a consequence we seek to avoid at all costs.

Divorcing Your Defects

As you contemplate the defects you'd like removed, make a list of each defect you are willing to claim as yours. After every defect, jot down the worst case scenario that might happen if that particular defect were to be removed. Now itemize the advantages to you of keeping the defect in your life. After that note the disadvantages — what negative impact does the defect or imbalance have on your life? Analyze whether or not the worst thing that could happen to you is a remote possibility or a probability. If it happened, could you, at this point in your development survive it? Finally, ask yourself whether or not you're willing to release each defect, and write a yes or no in the appropriate place.

Your worksheet might look something like this:

Defect: Don't stand up for myself or say what I want.

Worst Case Scenario: Husband yells at me and leaves me (unlikely that he'll leave, just threatens).

Advantages: Keeps the peace. I don't have to hear yelling. I'm not alone.

Disadvantages: Muscle tension. I feel sad and neglected 100% of the time.

Willing To Release?: Yes, because I feel like I'm dying inside. (I want to release this one in small steps!)

Now go over each of the shortcomings you have decided
to keep for the present and evaluate the feared consequences, for instance, twisted thinking — the maximizing,
minimizing and all-or-nothing thinking. Take time, days
or even weeks if you need, to meditate on your decision to
hang on to certain defenses. In the meantime, you might
try asking your Higher Power to help you let go of your
need to cling to old habits and to give you the strength
and courage to decide to face life without them.

As we approach the end of Step Six and feel that we are
entirely ready for our Higher Power to remove our defects
of character, a physical affirmation of our commitment
can be a way to mark our important decision. You might
choose to write your character defects down on slips of
paper, then burn them to symbolize their uselessness to
you and your detachment from them. Another way to
symbolically express your willingness to divorce your defects is to take some quiet time alone and reaffirm your
release of each shortcoming aloud.

Whenever we give anything up or have anything taken
from us be it a friendship, a love relationship, a habit like
smoking or even a ragged self-image, we experience grief.
We grieve over the loss of innocence, unhappy childhoods
and destructive illusions.

"No one ever told me that grief felt so like fear," wrote C.S.
Lewis after the death of his wife. To ignore the very real
necessity of the mourning process and act with bravado,
often sends us running to retrieve what we've given up
or to find a substitute for it in order to quiet the fear we
won't admit.

Our grief is a time of healing and of opening ourselves
to new ways of living. Although our first reaction to
becoming entirely ready to have our defects removed in
Step Six may be one of euphoria and relief, chances are it
will be followed by some sadness as we anticipate our
losses, realizing that not only are we giving up our imbalances, we are giving up our relationships to them, the
roles we've played for most of our lives. Even if we

remain with our partner, we are relinquishing our role as victim. This grieving follows a predictable pattern. If we understand that sequence of emotions, it will be easier for us to survive.

Reactions To Defect Losses

Our first reaction to the expected loss of our defects is often shock and numbness. We may walk around for a time in a daze wondering how this could be happening to us. We may sense that in being willing to let go of our shortcomings, we have passed a point of no return, that knowing what we now know and feeling what we now feel, we can never live exactly the way we did before. We can literally feel that the rug (the foundation of our defense system) has been pulled out from under us. We lose our footing.

When we regain our balance, typically we begin to feel a great deal of anger. We resent having wasted years of our lives listening to and believing the insults we heard. We may develop a short fuse and become irritable at things and events which normally wouldn't bother us. We go through a period of intense anger at ourselves for cooperating with the men we loved in their verbal dance of shame and rage. At this stage we ask ourselves how we could have been so stupid and short-sighted to take the emotional abuse and in some cases encourage it without ever trying to change the destructive patterns of our lives.

Once the anger abates, we go through a period of sadness and yearning. This is the time when we spend hours living in the past or trying to predict the future. Our favorite line of reasoning at this time becomes, "If only I'd done things differently . . . If only I could have been a better doormat . . . If only I didn't have any feelings . . . If only I'd been a better person . . ." We dwell on the good times in our relationship and fantasize how great it could be, if only he'd see the light and change, or we dwell on how wonderful a new relationship would be.

Fortunately, since we've come so far already in healing

from abusive relationships, the sadness and longing is only a temporary phase.

Soon we reach a stage of what grief counselors call apathy and loss of interest in life. Although these words have negative connotations, this stage of our process is a positive one. In effect, we're detaching, withdrawing into our inner world for a while to recharge our psychic batteries. We may sleep more and cut back on social engagements. While it may look to others as if we're in a holding pattern, in fact, there is a great deal going on beneath the surface, as in the roots of plants during the cold quiet of winter. We, too, are preparing for spring.

If we use this time to learn how to minimize life's stresses and to nourish ourselves, it will be wisely spent. We might find ourselves drawn to meditation or soft forms of exercise, like yoga or Tai Chi. We learn that it is not so bad to be alone sometimes, that we really enjoy a quiet walk through the woods by ourselves or an hour doing nothing but listening to our favorite music on the stereo. Because we've lived on the outside for so long, for others and through others, our retreat gives us a chance to be with ourselves, perhaps for the first time. Certainly, if this period of withdrawal lasts for too long or turns into depression, we may need professional help to find our way out. For most of us, however, temporary solitude is a major step toward finding inner peace.

Finally, as we approach Step Seven, we move into the reorganization phase. We discover the space left by our released shortcomings filling with more positive, constructive thoughts, feelings and actions. We come to know that we don't really need our defects and defense mechanisms in order to physically, emotionally or intellectually survive. In fact, we can be quite happy without their presence in our lives. We are ready with the help of our Higher Power to blossom.

> *I am completely ready and willing to untie the bonds of my character defects and hand them over to my Higher Power so that I may live and love more freely.*

10

Step Seven

We humbly asked our Higher Power
to remove our shortcomings.

*"Instead of wasting energy in being disgusted
with yourself, accept your own failures,
and just say to God, 'Well, in spite of all I may
say or fancy, this is what I am really like —
so please help my weakness.' This, not self-disgust,
is the real and fruitful humility."*

Evelyn Underhill

When we ask our Higher Power to remove our defects, instead of striving to eradicate them ourselves, we aren't giving up on becoming better people — we are admitting that we can't do it on our own. Our most tenacious efforts alone cannot make the deep and lasting changes we need in our lives. Too often when we attempt to live differently without the help of a Power outside of ourselves, the entirety of our energy is consumed in rooting up our defects and frantically trying to destroy them, only to find they've taken root again as fast as we can pull them up. We have little or no energy left with which to nurture ourselves and fill the empty spaces left by our weeding.

Because we are attempting to make broad and sweeping changes which go to the very core of our being (if we make this a do-it-yourself project), we stand a great chance of being overwhelmed. Transforming the basic ways we think, feel and act is not nearly as easy as losing ten pounds or learning to speak Swahili, both of which can be extremely difficult.

When we attempt a number of major changes alone, our lives quickly become a juggling act and we must constantly obsess on what we're doing to keep all the balls in the air at once. In the meantime, we may neglect the very practical demands on our time and energy — making house payments, raising children, even keeping our lives organized. Since we're human, we can only focus on so much at once or we drop the balls. Our desperate juggling act ends in failure.

Learning To Go With The Flow

The Seventh Step requires that we put our Higher Power in charge of the job of giving our lives balance. The only work we must do is to go with the flow, dealing with our resistance to the transformations God is working in our lives and trying our best to be cooperative with the process of change, rather than fighting it. Cooperating is no easy task. To meet this challenge and meet it well is demanding enough without taking on the additional job of bludgeoning ourselves into a spiritual, psychological and physical makeover.

The Seventh-Step process is not the same as booking emotional surgery to have our flaws removed, one where we are anesthetized while the doctor does it all. We are fully awake and aware the entire time. We do not have the luxury of removing ourselves from the mainstream of life while we're being "worked on." The transformation is an ongoing series of events, often a slow one, which allows us to let loose the tormented and often doomed-to-fail struggle to change, and guarantees that our changes will take place at the pace that's tailored for us — if we don't resist.

Sometimes we grow impatient when we don't see results happening right away. We want to magically be all better right now. We think our Higher Power has forgotten us so like frustrated children we yank and tug at the pieces of our lives, trying to fit them together by sheer will. Such willfulness when it arises stands as a barrier to discovering the path our Higher Power has in mind for us.

Some of us may associate the word "humility" in the Seventh Step with the groveling and cringing we did as targets of an emotional abuser. When we allow ourselves to be subservient to other human beings, we *are* unnecessarily giving up dignity and power over our lives. However, when we humble ourselves before the Divine, instead of diminishing our dignity, we increase it. The more control we give to our Higher Power, the less we allow other people to dominate us. We are simply admitting that we are humans and cannot possibly know everything that is best for us or carry it out. We are not miracle workers.

Many of our deficiencies, we couldn't remedy alone, no matter how hard we tried. There is no way we can go back to fill the gaps in our childhood with love, but our Higher Power can. We may not even be sure what love is until our Higher Power shows us. We can't find a magic solvent to wipe away our fear of intimacy. Our Higher Power can and will if we let it happen. Even though it is impossible for us to retreat and rewrite the sad and painful histories which brought us to the point we are at today, letting our Higher Power take charge, working through us and in us, can cause miraculous changes to happen in our lives.

Gradually allowing change to happen without pushing it, teaches us patience and helps us to incorporate our new way of looking at and dealing with life. This integration of the new with the functional parts of the old helps us to remain who we are. How disconcerting it would be to wake up one morning a totally new person with radically different thoughts, feelings, habits and interests than we had the night before. How confusing for those with whom we share our lives! Since few of us can afford to move to another country, change our name and take on a completely new identity, and since few of us would want to do that if we could, we have no other workable choice but to be fully receptive and gear ourselves to the slow steady transformation taking place inside ourselves.

Because it does take place deep inside, the results may not always be evident in our external perceptions. Rest assured that as long as you remain committed to releasing your defects and letting your Higher Power remove them for you, there is a great deal going on beneath your surface. Even when you aren't consciously thinking about it, the forces of change are at work, preparing you to act harmoniously with the universe in more enlightened ways. Trust isn't always easy to give, but it is essential for the Seventh Step to work.

As we enter this period of change, it is critical to focus our intentions on ourselves. When we try to transform ourselves so that others will like us, our gains are transitory. No matter how much we might want the people around us, especially our emotionally abusive mates, to undergo a transformation, we cannot make it happen. Neither should we focus our energies on begging our Higher Power to force our partners to change. But when we concentrate on our own defects and allow ourselves to be changed, ironically, we find that those around us change as well.

Systems Theory

Therapists explain this puzzling phenomena in terms of systems theory. Our interactions with others, especially in marriage and family relationships, make up a system. The sum effect of a particular system is greater than the total of its parts or the individuals who make it up. When one person in a system changes, acting in new ways, the other members are forced to behave differently if they wish to remain a part of the system. The transformation we allow to take place in our lives has a ripple effect, much like a stone dropped into a still pond. The waves such a change make are far-reaching and wash over the entire surface of the pool.

It is impossible to predict exactly how others, especially our partners, will respond to our new way of relating to life. Often in the beginning the people around us become threatened when they see us acting in unexpected ways. The more intimate we are with them and the more significant we are in their lives, the more resistance they will show. We're rocking the boat, making waves in the old familiar system and even though we may not intend to frighten others, they nonetheless become extremely wary of what we're doing.

Since emotional and psychological abusers are insecure people to begin with, their reaction to our refusal to play the game can be especially protracted and intense. They may respond with pleas that they liked us so much better the way we were. They may threaten to leave us or insult us, stepping up the intensity of the verbal assaults to a pitch they've never reached before. We may find that the men we live with try to sabotage our progress.

If we fight them or put our own needs aside to try to please them, we hook back into the old pattern — seeking approval and living outside ourselves through others, rather than paying the necessary attention to what we're feeling and needing. Certainly it is a good idea to be open about your intent to change and not be secretive. On the other hand, lengthy explanations are unnecessary and often futile. Often all they serve to do is to deplete your store of courage and weaken your resolve to let go and let God.

If your partner becomes so resistant to the changes you are allowing into your life that he threatens physical abuse or actually does slap, hit or otherwise assault you, it is important to protect yourself by leaving the scene immediately. There is nothing to be gained by remaining with a physically violent man and trying to talk sense into him or trying to get him to see things your way. Find a women's crisis center or another place you can stay and seek professional counseling to determine your options and to decide whether or not you really want to stay in the relationship any longer.

Will The Relationship End?

Some women find that the Seventh Step marks the end of their relationship. He may walk out because he's unwilling to live with the woman you're becoming. Being left is painful, even if you've wished he'd walk out for years. It is important to know that you can't force him to stay in the relationship if he doesn't want to. Neither can you make him love you if he doesn't want to. It is your right to change and it's his right not to like the changes and to terminate the relationship. To beg or plead with him only sets up a situation for worse psychological and verbal abuse than before.

It's possible, too, that you may be the one who decides the fabric of the relationship has been ripped beyond repair. This can be painful as well. Even though you are giving the relationship up, rather than having it taken from you, there is still a grieving process to work through. It is not easy to make a decision of such far-reaching consequences.

When our relationships end as a direct result of our unwillingness to accept emotional abuse as something we deserve or need, we still hurt. Through the hurt, we need to keep in mind that not all of the changes the Higher Power works in our lives are necessarily ones we would have chosen for ourselves. Nonetheless they are for our greater good. Often our losses are simply a way to clear a space for something better to occur in our lives than we ever expected would happen. Because we can't foresee the future, we may grow unnecessarily insecure and frightened. This is the time to concentrate on our relationship to the Divine and to seek comfort from the assurance it brings us.

As we change we need to be mindful that not everyone is going to be as excited about what is happening inside of us as we are, and we need to resist the temptation of zealotry. Our purpose is to allow the Higher Power to work through us, not to convert everyone we know to our new way of thinking.

When we stand on a soapbox and spread the new-found word, not only do we risk thoroughly turning people off, we tend to use our mission as a way to distance ourselves from what is occurring inside of us. It becomes much easier to talk about changing than to actually foster an environment where change will happen. We need to remember that the transformation of our own hearts, minds and spirits is a more powerful testimony to the power of the Twelve Steps than any amount of lecturing or cajoling we can do.

Often the reaction of others to the removal of our defects is the least of our worries — we have enough to do just keeping ourselves open and receptive to that removal. Without thinking we may slide back into old patterns of thinking and behaving. Under stress we may clutch frantically at our old defenses. At times we become discouraged and want to give up. Sometimes we may backslide so far and so consistently, it seems we are taking two steps backward for every one we take forward.

Passive resistance to change is part of the human condition. None of us is a candidate for sainthood yet. With the help of our Higher Power, we are unlearning an old way of living and learning a new one. Learning curves are never smooth. Sometimes we reach plateaus where we stop for a while to catch our breaths and assimilate what we're learning. At other times we slide back a bit. It is quite possible that a step or two in a backward direction is necessary for us to test whether or not the changes we are making are really useful. We may slide back into old behaviors for a short time as a way to check whether or not we really do want to change. More often than not after a short period of going back to our old ways, we're ready to accept further change with a higher degree of renewed commitment to let our Higher Power take charge.

Self-Sabotage

At other times we may actively resist change in ourselves and battle with our Higher Power, verbalizing an intent to be open to change but actually closing our hearts to the transformation, working to thwart it at every turn. When we become aware of this tendency to sabotage our progress, we can put the brakes on our backsliding before we regress too far. As with any addictive behavior, compulsively relating to people who emotionally abuse us is a temptation. It will always be a temptation.

If we are not aware of that tendency within ourselves, we set ourselves up for a full-blown relapse. We reconnect with the partners we left or who left us. We try to undo the positive changes which are occurring in our current relationships, turning them back into abusive ones. We may even seek out new partners who know the steps to the dance of emotional abuse, and establish relationships with them. When this happens, we may blame our Higher Power when, in truth, it was our own willfulness and closed-mindedness which caused our downfall.

When such downfalls happen, when we hook back into patterns of emotional abuse, we need to turn it around to live in harmony with our Higher Power's intent and with the Twelve Steps. The longer we remain committed to change, the weaker the temptation to live according to our old habits. When we can detach enough from our internal process to examine the ways we thwart change and fight our Higher Power, we are on the road to mastery and actively avoiding a repeat of our past.

One of the most common ways we sabotage ourselves is to set unrealistic goals. Either they are too large and broad in scope or we project consequences of our changes more in the light of fairy tales than real life. Because of our perfectionism and all-or-nothing thinking, we may decide that if we don't make all the changes we want immediately or if they aren't of the magnitude we want them to be, we have failed or our Higher Power has.

We hook unrelated outcomes to our goals. For instance, we might imagine that once we are able to give and receive sexual intimacy, we'll be multi-orgasmic or that once we stop living out the role of victim, no one will ever be angry with us again.

When we succumb to this way of thinking, we realize that we're usurping the job of directing our recovery from our Higher Power. Our unrealistic expectations blind us to the very real changes which are happening in our lives. Since we're always looking for our preconceived dreams of the future to occur, we shift our gaze from the here and now to some distant image of bliss. We need to reconcile ourselves to living our recovery one day or even one minute at a time and take joy in the positives that are happening rather than wasting energy worrying about the future.

Another way we sabotage our Higher Power's efforts and set ourselves up for backsliding is to put ourselves in situations where temptation is greater than normal. Early on in our recovery, especially, we may need to withdraw from circumstances which trigger our victim stance instead of "testing" ourselves by having much contact with emotionally abusive people. We tell ourselves that one little conversation with a macho man who treats us like an object isn't going to hurt, then we suddenly find ourselves dating him or even living with him. Giving in on just one argument and sacrificing our own self-esteem isn't going to hurt us, we tell ourselves, then we give in to two or three or four. Suddenly our lives are back where they started.

Often when we wake up to reality, we use the same twisted logic to stay stuck as a dieter who eats just one chocolate chip cookie and finishes off the whole batch. Since she's already ruined her diet, she tells herself, she might as well go on an eating binge. When we backslide and get away from the program, we need to catch our-

selves quickly, and rather than beating ourselves up emotionally and spiritually, we must get ourselves back on
track as quickly as possible.

The Poison Of Negative Thinking

Probably the most poisonously potent method of self-
sabotage we can use is to emotionally abuse ourselves by
practicing negative thinking. We tell ourselves that no
matter what our Higher Power does, we just aren't capable of changing. When we experience successes, we
tell ourselves we don't deserve them. We inform ourselves that since our lives are doomed to be messy failures
anyway and since there's no hope for terrible and weak
people like ourselves, we might as well give up and go
back to our old ways.

This negative brainwashing is a result of trying to second
guess our Higher Power and in effect play God. When we
make negative judgments about ourselves, when we punish
ourselves for being ourselves, we insult the Divine who
created us. Often our negative thinking and indulging in
shame is only a cover for our unwillingness to change.
When we feel self-pity, we are usually really yearning to go
back to our familiar bad habits and giving ourselves an
excuse to indulge in that old destructive behavior.

Sometimes when we're unrealistic about the change we
want to see in our lives, when we put ourselves in dangerously tempting circumstances or when we indulge in self-
pity, it is enough to renew our commitment to allow our
Higher Power to remove our defects, then get on with the
business of our recovery. At other times, we need to take
quick remedial action, reworking past steps to correct our
course and get back on the right track.

Many women have found that Twelve-Step support
groups provide positive feedback as they let go of their
defects and let God restore balance to their lives. Not
only does sharing our concerns and our issues with others of like mind and purpose give us moral support, but
we're able to view the transformations taking place in
the lives of others and get a more accurate picture of

what we can expect. Interacting with other women allows us to see that progress doesn't happen in a straight line, that it may happen slowly, but it happens all the same. By observing the growth taking place in others, the knowledge that there is hope for us is reinforced. Such positive support networks can also serve as an antidote for negative relationships.

Visualizations And Affirmations

Creative visualization is another technique which works for many women as a substitute for negative thinking and self-sabotage. Because our minds and memory banks don't distinguish between fantasy experiences and real ones, it is possible to program ourselves with the positive, by creating clear and vivid mental images of ourselves living fulfilled and balanced lives. By mentally rehearsing positive changes we make ourselves more receptive to them and integrate them more quickly when they occur. Many good books are available which teach visualization. It is important as we learn the technique and practice it that we use images generated in conjunction with our Higher Power rather than falling into the trap of imposing our wills on the cosmic design.

Finally, verbal affirmations can be a powerful tool for the positive to fill our lives and spirits. We can find affirmations like the ones at the end of each chapter in this book or we can learn to write our own. The key guidelines for writing affirmations is that they be short and simple, that they be framed in positive language and that they affirm our desire to follow the will of our Higher Power. Phrasing our affirmations in the present tense makes them more immediate.

As we experiment with techniques to open ourselves to transformation, we need to rely on the inspiration and guidance of our Higher Power, leaning on that source, not only to change us, but to help us accept and assimilate the change. The knowledge, support and help we need will be revealed to us. All we must do is to take quiet time alone to communicate with our Higher Power, increasing our receptivity to Divine direction for our lives.

> *I am learning to listen to my Higher Power — and listening to learn. My Higher Power is restoring balance to my life daily. All I need do is cooperate.*

11

❧

Step Eight

We made a list of all persons we had harmed and
became willing to make amends to them all.

*"I learned that true forgiveness included total
acceptance. And out of acceptance wounds are
healed and happiness is possible again."*

Catherine Marshall

Everybody makes mistakes but women enmeshed in
verbally and emotionally violent relationships tend to
forget that important fact of life. Emotionally abusive
relationships are based on blame and shame. Our verbally
abusing partners transform their own shame or lack of
self-acceptance into rage and heave it at us. We in turn
accept their shame and add it to our already large burden
of self-loathing.

We, too, begin to blame our partners for everything
that goes wrong with our lives, and become manipulative,
harming others under the guise of doing things for their
own good.

Shame

If we are honest, many of us will admit to dragging around huge sacks laden with shame most of our lives. That's how we came to be trapped in dysfunctional relationships with men in the first place. We were ashamed of ourselves and felt we deserved every insult and indignity our partners flung our way. We often settled for the first interested man who came along because we didn't think we were worthy of someone who respected us and treated us well.

With our newly found honesty and acceptance, we have diminished some of our shame at who we are. Chances are we still carry a great deal of that emotion from growing up with parents who shamed us. As we progressed, working the steps and finished doing our inventories, we may have begun to feel a sense of remorse over the bad decisions we've made and the wrong turns our lives have taken. When we finally admitted that we weren't martyred saints and therefore our partners weren't 100% sinners, our feelings of unworthiness may have seemed overwhelming.

Over time shame solidifies and cripples us from taking action. Because our self-esteem was already at a bedrock low when we were in emotionally abusive relationships, we may have found it difficult to admit our mistakes to ourselves, let alone to the people those mistakes had harmed. Our lives became a constant battle to put on good appearances for the outside world. When we said or did hurtful things and didn't acknowledge them, the guilt we felt didn't go away. Instead it grew and hardened into even more shame as we forgot we'd done this or that "horrible" thing and felt only that we were "horrible" people.

Sifting Through Shame And Guilt

The Eighth Step helps us to sift through our shame and begin to do something about it. We start to focus on what we did, rather than what perfectly miserable wretches we think we are. In order to convert shame back into guilt we feel remorse for our actions rather than our essence, thereby reversing the shame-formation process. After we've enumerated and confronted the instances in which our behavior and patterns of relating have harmed others, we are ready to let go of our guilt by moving to the Ninth Step — making amends to the people we have harmed both knowingly and unintentionally. As we face our shame and guilt head-on and work through it, we are once more able to move freely, no longer hobbled by the past.

Before we can become willing to let go of our burden though, we must be able to understand that even while it suffocated us and prevented us from truly living our lives to their fullest, our guilt and shame also served us well as defenses. When we believe that we are terrible people worthy of punishment and that no matter how hard we try we can't do anything right, we have absolutely no motivation to try a different, more positive style of relating. When we're closely aligned and identified with shame, we don't have to take real responsibility for the things we say and do. After all, we're terrible people so we can't do any better than we're doing. Our guilt over our past actions paralyzes us and we have the perfect excuse not to act in the future. In effect our disability becomes a blessing in disguise — an excuse for every one of our shortcomings, a reason to keep ourselves stagnating and out of the mainstream of life.

Facing Self-Pity And Resentment

When we carry them around long enough, our guilt and shame turn into resentments. Self-pity isn't a pleasant emotion. We're prone to ease our discomfort by blaming others for our dreary emotional states. We forget that we have the power to accept or to reject shame — that as adults, nobody can force us to feel a way we do not choose to feel. We forget that, in the case of the guilt we carry over things we've done or haven't done, our actions, not the reactions of others, provoked the stab of conscience in the first place. If we ignore that stab as a signal to mend our ways, we give ourselves permission to persist in

harmful and disharmonious actions and to keep feeling
self-pity and resentment.

Often the resentments, which have been breeding in
the stagnant swamp of self-pity, spur us to take revenge
on people in subtle and not so subtle ways. We may
indirectly express our anger at our partner by never
wanting to have sex, "forgetting" to keep a promise or
developing a learned incompetence which keeps us from
being responsible and capable people. Instead of solving
our problems, our vengeful subterfuge makes them
worse. Because on some level we know we're being dishonest and manipulative, our actions create more guilty
feelings for us to carry around.

When we can't get back at our partners or we're too
afraid to, we may take our anger out on people who can't
or won't fight back. Our tempers flare at our children
over minor infractions. We may feel a thrill at carrying
tales and gossiping about co-workers because it gives us
power in lives we view as powerless. We may complain
and try to burden friends with our problems, then become
angry when they make suggestions. We might flirt with
other women's husbands and attempt to lure them away
from their marriages so that we can feel attractive. Or we
begin affairs only to break them off in anger when we
discover the new men in our lives can't fix our flagging
self-esteem. Without being completely aware of what
we're doing, we take revenge against a world we feel has
dealt us an unjust hand.

Killing With Kindness

Many times we harm people while harboring the best
of intentions. One of the most common reasons women in
abusive relationships do this is to protect others from the
consequences of their own actions. Because we have a
strong need to take care of the people close to us, we may
cover up a spouse's drinking or a teenage child's drug-
taking. Although we may know our kids didn't do their
homework, we go to bat for them with their teachers,
sometimes going so far as to lie to save them from failing.

At our jobs we find ourselves doing other peoples' work and allowing them to take the credit.

Even when our partners, our children, our friends and our co-workers know that what they've done is wrong and take steps to apologize or correct their mistakes, we convince them otherwise. "That's okay," we'll say, "It was really my fault." Or "You couldn't help yourself." In this way we deny them responsibility for their actions and keep them tied to us, dependent on us to rescue them from their misbehavior. In short, we are harming them even when we may feel our most self-righteous and appear our kindest.

As we work Step Eight we need to take a careful look at *all* our relationships, even the ones which are no longer current. In order to do a thorough shame and guilt house-cleaning, we must go back to the beginning. Often the list of those we have harmed is less difficult to do if we work on it in chronological order, starting with our earliest memories and trying to think of the people we knew at various times in our lives.

The most effective way to make the list is to do a rough draft first, brainstorming as many of our transgressions as possible, even if on the surface they appear trivial. The purpose of this first list is to generate raw material and to get us thinking. Often an entry which seems silly at first glance will unlock another memory of an incident we've suppressed, but one which we still feel guilty about.

Your first list might be comprised of early entries something like these:

1. Caused my parents to divorce by being born.
2. Put gum in my little sister's hair and said she'd done it — she was punished.
3. Stole a pen from the drug store in third grade.
4. Cheated on math tests in jr. high.
5. Lied to my parents about going out with my friends.
6. Put a dent in the fender of the family car when I was learning to drive.
7. Forgot to clean my room sometimes.

When you've finished this preliminary list covering your pre-adult years, reread it and analyze the list, placing a check by the items which did not harm other people and those which were really out of your control. For instance, when you were younger, you may have been told your parents would never have divorced if you hadn't been born, but in truth you didn't ask to be born. The shame or guilt you carry for that is not yours because by no stretch of the imagination can an infant "make" adults end a relationship. Your parents chose to have you and your parents chose to divorce. Perhaps you were blamed for their decisions, but now as an adult you have a choice to reject that blame and let go of the type of magical thinking that says children have the power to make or break their parents' lives.

Lying, cheating and stealing are acts which harm others, but putting a dent in the car and forgetting to clean your room are fairly typical teenage behaviors. The most important developmental task of growing up is making those mistakes and learning from them by trial and error. If we didn't make mistakes, how could we learn? We're all less than perfect — even as adults. Growing up in a dysfunctional family we learned that we weren't supposed to make any mistakes — ever — and that we had to be perfect in order to be accepted. As time went on we adopted these impossible standards and internalized them. We learned to feel shame and guilt about very normal and natural characteristics and acts. Just being a five-year-old or a seven-year-old or a thirteen-year-old was enough to disappoint or anger our parents. Years later we may agonize over the transgressions of our childhood only to find that when we examine them, they reflect healthy behavior. Place a check next to the items on your list which were generated by perfectionism and those which did not harm you or other people.

Forgiving Your Inner Child

When you've finished, try to visualize yourself as a child. If this is difficult, dig out an old picture of you when you were younger. Imagine that this child, who is you, is sitting next to you, quietly listening to what you have to say to her. Now forgive her for each of the items you've checked, instances where you made mistakes that didn't harm others, where you angered or disappointed parents by simply being a normally developing child or failed to meet unreasonably high goals. Tell her it's okay to be herself, that you love and accept her for who she is no matter what she's done or failed to do. Let her know that you love her and acknowledge that she's a part of you, even though you are now an adult.

Working through the inheritance of shame we didn't deserve takes time. You will probably need to talk to your little girl and reassure her again and again that you are glad she was born, that you love her and that it is okay if she makes mistakes. Each time you do, you move closer and closer to self-acceptance and self-forgiveness. The burden of shame grows lighter and you are more able to honestly face the times where you wittingly or unwittingly harmed others with your actions.

Forgiving The Adult Child

It is now time to deal with our adult years. This time as you make your preliminary brainstorming list, continue to do so chronologically, but break it into categories, dealing with one type of relationship at a time. As you write you may begin to see patterns emerging.

For instance, most of the hurtful things you've done or said may focus in one or two areas of your life or you may discover that over the years, you've honed two or three methods of hurting others to razor-sharp efficiency. You might be an expert at laying guilt trips on people or subtly undercutting their self-esteem. Perhaps you tend to play two people against each other, egging them on from the sidelines. This awareness of what you've done is an essential step toward change. Until we know our harmful tendencies and techniques, we have no way of knowing what to release and make amends for.

Too often we've felt guilty about how we made people around us feel and, at the same time, have ignored the real harm we've caused others. We are not responsible for the times when others feel angry, disappointed or sad, just as we can't force other people to be happy. On the other hand, the impact of our words and actions can be destructive, provoking conflicts, chipping away at the self-esteem of others or providing them with false information so that their lives are based on illusion rather than reality. Even though we don't force other people to feel certain ways, we do set up situations which tend to evoke those feelings. When we get caught up in being sorry for *ourselves* because we always "make" other people rage or cry or dislike us, rather than being sorry for and correct-ing our *actions*, we evade accepting the core truth that we harm people with specific words and actions, not by simply existing. We avoid responsibility and growth.

The following areas are ones you'll want to explore as you begin your preliminary list of people you have know-ingly and unknowingly harmed. By no means, are these ways of harming others complete — they are merely idea joggers to get you moving. By the same token, you prob-ably won't have done every single thing detailed. Still, you may discover that you've hurt someone in a similar fash-ion. The task at hand right now is to make your own unique list which accurately reflects *your* life as you've lived it so far, not to construct a case study.

Men In Previous And Current Relationships

Because so many of us depend on men to fix us or to bolster our low self-esteem, we may collect them, only to toss them aside when they're used up, then go on to find another. We may treat men as objects rather than as feeling human beings. Other women may cling to partners long after the relationship is over, begging them to stay and harassing them after they leave, in effect trying to rob them of their freedom of choice.

Some of us mother the men we're with, emasculating them by taking care of them and fostering feelings of incompetence. We may take over the emotional dealings in our families, never allowing the men we love to develop tenderness or to nurture because we feel that relationship maintenance is women's work.

Perhaps we manage the men we live with, doing countless little unasked-for favors, which have the cumulative effect of running their lives and engendering a huge debt of gratitude which we expect someday to collect. Often emotionally abused women have difficulty accepting presents or even compliments, preferring instead to give and give, thus accumulating yet more debts of gratitude.

When we team up with partners who have few employment skills, are chemically dependent or emotionally troubled, we many times fall into the trap of rescuer, saving them from themselves. While this role can make us feel needed and wanted, it prevents our partners from learning to face their own problems and from taking charge of their own lives. We complain that they act like little boys, but are threatened when they act as adults so we do everything within our power to keep them tied to our apron strings.

Because of our own ambivalent feelings about intimacy, we may alternate between clinging and pushing partners away, one minute expecting them to fill our every need and the next isolating and distancing ourselves. We often have difficulty expressing our wants, needs and feelings, but at the same time expect the men we love to read our minds. We may become bitter and blame them for their incompetence when they can't guess at what we want and provide it. We might become experts at self-protection by giving mixed messages, even to the point of contradicting ourselves in the space of a few words so that nobody can take offense at what we say. Such crazy-making behavior can spur our partners to doubt their own competence and even their own sanity.

Frequently we volunteer to act as doormats, then become outraged when our partners wipe their feet on us. We blame them for everything that goes wrong in our lives instead of looking inside and honestly asking ourselves if we have contributed to the genesis of the problem. Too often we punish our partners by withholding affection or sex. We may also rule our relationships by guilt, telling the men we love they have no right to feel the way they do after all we've done for them. We often manipulate so that their guilt after an outburst is used as permission for a shopping spree or another indulgence we'd normally avoid in our martyr crusade.

Co-dependency harms both the co-dependent and the person she is dependent upon. Whether we are addicted to men or to a single man, we cease to view our partners as individuals. Instead, they become things — a means to the end of raising our self-esteem and making ourselves feel better. The more dependent we become upon others for emotional support and the less we are able to provide that support for ourselves, the more we dehumanize those we claim to love. That dehumanization — turning a person into an object and using that object to meet our needs — hurts our partners as well as ourselves.

Children

As we discussed earlier, emotional and verbal violence tends to filter through families from the top down, from the most powerful to the most powerless. Some of us have maintained relationships with men who verbally or even physically or sexually abused our children. Because we were addicted to our partners and believed we needed them in order to survive, we turned a blind eye to the abuse they perpetrated on our children.

Others passed the verbal and emotional abuse down the power chain. Because we were angry at being victimized, we acted as aggressors with our kids, insulting them, manipulating them and invading their physical and emotional boundaries in an attempt to control every area of their lives. Because they were children, smaller than we and less mature, they couldn't fight back.

Even when we've made the supreme effort to protect our children from the abusive outbursts of our partners and to keep ourselves from being psychologically violent, we still have helped to create a dysfunctional family system with many of the same rules which set *us* up to be victims. We've taught our children not to express their true feelings and, in some cases, not even to feel them in the first place. We've shown them that promises are made to be broken and that people aren't to be trusted. They've learned from us that conflict is to be avoided at all costs.

Our sons and daughters have learned to devalue women from our example. We've modeled a negative and destructive relationship for them and have tried to pass it off as being normal. In our isolation and our desire to keep our emotionally abusive relationship a secret from the world, we may have deliberately isolated our kids or neglected to teach them rudimentary social skills. They now have a difficult time making friends. We taught them with our denial that truth and honesty aren't important qualities.

As long as we remained in an emotionally abusive relationship and tried to control the man who abused us, we placed that man in the center of our lives. From what they've seen of our lives, our kids may have come to equate love with abuse. While our energy and attention revolved around the psychological abuser, we may have neglected the emotional and even the physical needs of our children. Their problems and concerns seemed trivial compared to ours. Their needs had to be sacrificed, so we told ourselves, in order to keep the peace.

Many of us have found ourselves manipulating our kids with the same harmful and dehumanizing techniques we've used on our spouses. We may be coercive, provoke guilt or expect our children to emotionally parent us. Although we may not yell at them or hit them, our undercover manipulations can be just as damaging, perhaps more so because they are nearly impossible to directly confront.

Growing up in a home where emotional abuse is a daily or weekly fact of life is harmful to children, even though they may not have been direct targets of that abuse.

Despite the fact we thought we were protecting our children, we have been tutoring them to be victims or perpetrators of verbal and psychological violence themselves. By expecting them to deny reality along with their feelings, to be compliant and to always put the needs of others before their own, we have done them great harm.

Friends, Extended Family And Co-workers

We rarely stop using the destructive techniques we have used to cope with emotional abuse when we leave our nuclear family. Since so many of us learned those harmful skills in our family of origin, we continue to relate in old maladaptive ways with brothers and sisters, as well as with our parents. We may trade in secrets and gossip to increase our power, persisting in gossiping about one to another. We may encourage people to take our side in a conflict and urge them to fight our battles for us.

Perhaps we play out the martyr role to the hilt at family gatherings and at the office, making all the sacrifices and doing all of the dirty work, meanwhile simmering with resentment. We may find passive ways to get back at bosses because they remind us of our parents or our spouses. Or perhaps we stifle our anger, putting on a placid front and then exploding at the slightest provocation.

Many of us find ourselves so caught in denial that we have a difficult time telling the truth about anything. Our lack of honesty is evident when we use our spouse as an excuse for not doing our work or for breaking promises. We give our friends and co-workers mixed messages or we expect them to read our minds and become embittered when they "fail" us. Some of us evolve into complainers who invariably have something negative to say about everything or everybody.

We might expect our friends to solve our problems, dropping everything to come to our rescue. Or we may become bossy managers, telling them how to run their lives and trying to keep them dependent so they won't abandon us. When people become too close, we often panic and abruptly end the relationship without ever giving an explanation or with loud and long blaming of the other person for the friendship's demise.

All of these behaviors leave hurt, anger and confusion in their wake. Even when we haven't set out to harm members of our extended family, our co-workers and our friends, our way of relating to the world may have diminished rather than added to the lives of those we've met. As we look back, we need to recall those instances where we brought negativity to others by our words and our deeds.

Checking Our Lists

When your list is complete, reread it carefully, crossing out and forgiving yourself for times you either didn't harm others or had accepted someone else's blame and shame. When you are finished, you should have a list composed of specific and concrete behaviors and the people you have harmed. At this point, it may be obvious that most of the instances in which we hurt others, we also manage to hurt ourselves. Even if we escape harm in the short run, it catches up to us in the long run.

Take some time to add to your list the things you've done which were self-destructive in and of themselves and not necessarily as a consequence of harming others. You are a person and you count just as much as the others on your list. Overeating, addictive drinking, tranquilizer abuse and excessive smoking fall into this category. So do other behaviors like emotionally beating yourself up for being less than perfect or holding your anger inside until you develop physical aches and pains.

Once we've honestly accepted the impact our shortcomings have had on others, we are asked to become willing to make amends to all the people (including ourselves) we have harmed. We must release our destructive ways of relating to other people and let go of our need for revenge. Some of us find it very difficult to stop emotionally killing others with kindness, and we find it isn't easy to give up our burden of shame. We're so used to living with it, we're afraid we can't function without it.

Losing our shame and our guilt are like any other losses. We grieve over what we no longer have, no matter how disgusted we are with what we're giving up. As we mourn the familiar old us, we come to a new understanding and acceptance of ourselves and we heal. We learn that "no man is an island" and that what we say and what we do affects those around us. Just as we chose to have a negative impact, we can choose to have a positive one. Just as we made mistakes which harmed others, we can rectify those mistakes and learn to live without shame and perpetual remorse.

I fully acknowledge that through my words, my actions and my lack of action, I have harmed other people and myself. I am completely willing to make amends to the others I have harmed and to myself.

12

❦

Step Nine

We made direct amends to such people
whenever possible, except when to do so would
injure them or others.

*"One's philosophy is not best expressed in words,
it is expressed in the choices one makes."*

Eleanor Roosevelt

When we worked Step Eight, we assessed the nature and
the depth of our shame and guilt. We were able to rid
ourselves of the shameful feelings we did not deserve. In
Step Nine we take action to set our misdeeds straight and
to set our relationships with others on a new course. In the
process we can put much of our guilt behind us. Although
we can never completely undo the past, we can make every
attempt to make amends, thereby putting our former misdeeds where they belong — in the past. Once we can view
them as lessons, we can stop obsessing over them.

That is not to say we'll never feel guilt again. We will,
as we certainly ought to when we do wrong in the future.

In addition we will harm others at times simply because we are human beings and, therefore, imperfect. However, once we've done the work of Step Nine, we can make our amends quickly, rather than letting the guilt fester into shame because of timidity or a false sense of pride.

Step Nine stretches us, sometimes painfully so, in order that we can grow big enough to not only admit when we are wrong, but to take action to clean up our messes, rather than trying to hide them.

The requirement of making amends is much different than the half-hearted and ineffective strategies we have probably used in the past. Too often we overused the words, "I'm sorry," either to deflect the anger of others and save our own skins or to keep from rocking the boat.

"I'm sorry," we murmured when it rained and we couldn't take the kids on a picnic — as if the rain were our fault.

"I'm sorry," we whispered in bed when a lover couldn't get an erection — as if his sexual functioning were totally our responsibility.

"I'm sorry," we pleaded when we cooked pot roast and it turned out our partner wanted stew and hadn't expressed it.

Did we mean that litany of sorrow? If we're completely honest with ourselves, we must answer, "Absolutely not!" Although the phrase, "I'm sorry," may have had some initial meaning early in our lives, we repeated it so often, it became an empty chant which we spoke without thinking, sprinkling it into our conversations like a magical formula designed to ward off the evil eye and to keep our resentment hidden from others, even from ourselves.

Overcompensation

Neither is making amends the frantic overcompensation so many of us practiced when we sensed we had harmed others in the past. Often instead of directly owning up to our wrongs, we threw ourselves into a frenzy of making up to people for the grief we'd caused them. Some of us struggled to be all-loving and completely generous after we'd been crabby with our kids and denied one of their requests. We'd pull a 180-degree turn and shower them with presents, indulging their every whim — until the next time we lost our temper. We did the same thing with our partners, trying to compensate for being late or forgetting to pick up the dry-cleaning with a flurry of affection and special treats, only to snap back into our passivity or silence or crying when our resentments grew too much for us.

More often than not, our overcompensation didn't smooth the ruffled feathers anyway. Instead our erratic behavior caused even more hurt. Much of the time our overcompensation was completely out of proportion to the harm we'd caused. Sometimes we used it to punish or martyr ourselves in an attempt to secretly atone for our trangressions. Some of us overcompensated when we hadn't harmed others, but they were merely irritable or out of sorts, a condition we had little or nothing to do with causing. Like "I'm sorry," overcompensation became an automatic response to control the emotions of others.

The times our making up turned into self-punishment, it filled us with even more resentments and set us up to do further harm because we quickly forgot that we'd chosen to deny and punish ourselves, that it wasn't something our loved ones forced upon us. Sometimes our self-punishment wasn't even linked to directly rectifying our wrongs but instead became a magical ritual to be done in private. We'd stop eating for a day or isolate ourselves or deny ourselves the pleasure of listening to music or making love in order to even out the balance, to punish ourselves before others had the chance. We'd dress ourselves in drab colors or stop ourselves from buying a magazine we wanted to read. In time we came to believe that others had cast us in this martyr role and we may have become insufferably self-righteous. In the meantime, our wrongs were hidden beneath a thick layer of self-pity.

Because of the way we were raised and the off-kilter relationships we formed as adults, we may confuse making amends with making excuses. Whenever we perform a harmful act, whether it is intentional or unintentional, we feel a need to give our victims a detailed analysis of why we did what we did. We really couldn't help ourselves because we didn't know any better or we had a rotten childhood or we were just about to get our period. The more we explain and excuse ourselves, the further we get from correcting what we did that was hurtful.

Often our excuses grow to the point where although we start off by apologizing, we end up expecting our listeners to understand us and become quite angry when they don't or when they see through our subterfuge and confront us with our evasion of responsibility. As we explain, we grow convinced that we didn't have any option but to do what we did and we fall deeper into the trap of self-pity.

Reparations And Corrections

It is important for us to understand that Step Nine doesn't tell us to beg for forgiveness or to ask others to absolve us from our guilty feelings by understanding our motives. Forgiveness is something we must give ourselves and ask from our Higher Power. Our job is to make amends: reparations, corrections and improvements. When we can and when it will not further harm others, we must do whatever is possible to repair the damage we've caused and correct the relationship. In some instances, when we can't set our wrongs right, we must put the past behind us and take steps to improve that relationship in the future.

All this takes a great deal of acceptance. First we must accept the gravity of our wrongs and completely acknowledge the extent to which they've harmed others. Then we must accept our responsibility to straighten out the messes we've made. We must also accept that some of the hurt we've caused is irreversible, so we can only accept the consequences of our actions and learn to live with them without resentment or self-pity, no matter how uncomfortable we feel. Sometimes we simply must let bygones be bygones and stop picking at the wounds.

This is a time when the *Serenity Prayer* can offer a great deal of support as we ask our Higher Power to help us see the difference between the amends we can't make without creating further harm and those we wish to evade because of lack of inner courage.

> *God grant me the serenity*
> *to accept the things I cannot change.*
> *Courage to change the things I can.*
> *And wisdom to know the difference.*

Obviously, we can't make amends to people who we no longer have contact with and those who have died. Often many of the amends we must make which relate to the occurrences of childhood will fall under this heading. No matter how much we'd like to make reparations, circumstantially it is impossible.

Dealing With Secrets

In other instances, our transgressions were secret and openly acknowledging them would probably hurt people more than it would help them, especially if the harm we caused is not ongoing. For instance, revealing a past affair which has since ended may only stir up feelings of betrayal. In confessing affairs, too, we run the risk of damaging the lives and reputations of third parties. We need to be careful not to use Step Nine as an excuse to tell all, and in the act of unburdening ourselves, take revenge on the very people to whom we're making amends.

Sometimes making amends might lead to imprisonment, losing a job or other major crises. If this is the case, we need to weigh carefully the best course of action for us to take, asking our Higher Power for guidance. We might decide that the best way to make an amend for stealing from our place of employment would be to anonymously mail payment for what we took because to do otherwise would mean losing our job which is our means of supporting our children.

There is no hard and inflexible rule which we can apply to such situations. Sometimes, as in the case of using

illegal drugs, the only way to make amends without harming our family is to seek treatment and correct our behavior rather than calling the police and turning ourselves in.
The important question to ask ourselves in circumstances
like these is whether we are avoiding the consequences of
making amends because they are merely unpleasant or
avoiding them because they would create real and unnecessary harm for others who depend on us.

When it's impossible to make a direct amend, we need
to make an internal one, forgiving ourselves for what
we've done and resolving never again to repeat the harm
we've done. In these cases, our corrected actions become
our amends. Actions do speak more loudly than words.
While words may be very important in some instances,
they aren't always required — especially if they compound
the hurt we've done.

How we make amends to our children will vary with
their ages. Younger children may not fully comprehend a
verbal amend, but nonetheless, apologizing in words they
can understand is an important act for our own growth.
When they see that we acknowledge our wrongs and take
steps to correct them, they learn how to do that in their
own lives. We also need to show them that we are willing
to back our words with actions. If we've been overly
lenient or inconsistent with them, they may not like our
actions at first. We need to understand that making
amends is not a popularity contest.

If we feel shaky about our parenting skills, which is a
distinct possibility since so many of us were not parented
well, we may need to seek outside help, either through
parenting skills classes or family therapy as part of the
amends process toward our children. We can never go
back and undo the harm we've done, but we can admit
we've made mistakes and do everything within our power
to do better from now on. Part of the consequences of
our actions and lack of action may be that our children
will grow up to have difficulty with relationships when
they are teenagers or adults. As long as we don't hide our

errors from them and attempt a cover-up in order to protect our own image, they can learn to recognize and deal with problems when they arise.

Sometimes making direct amends to others may be inappropriate now, but possible at a later date. This is often true of the reparations we need to make to our emotionally and verbally abusive mates. If our partner's anger at us is at a high level, it isn't always wise to talk about what we've done wrong in the past, outside of the context of professional counseling, because it may do nothing but dredge up past grievances and provoke yet another emotionally abusive verbal attack. If you have reason to believe that in making a verbal amend, you'll only be providing ammunition which will be used against you in the future, you have the option of making a silent amend and working on changing your behavior, rather than talking about it.

Our partners may not even be willing to hear what we want to say to them, and they may balk at the very mention of going to counseling with us. When this happens, we have no choice but to let go and let God. We may decide that we do not want to wait for the situation to change; to delay would be emotionally damaging to us and to our children. If we do decide to remain in the relationship, we can work on changing our own behavior, giving up our attempts to control our partner's actions and feelings and, in that way, satisfying the requirements of Step Nine.

We may find as we begin to work amends, that in addition to being held back by our partner's anger or the anger of others we've wronged, our *own* resentment still stands in the way of making a clean confession of the wrong we've done and taking measures to right it. If your anger blocks you from progress, then it's time to retreat and rework steps Four, Five, Six and Seven, honestly admitting your anger to yourself, confessing it to your Higher Power and another human being, becoming willing to let it go, then asking your Higher Power to remove it. Making premature and, therefore, insincere amends does

more harm than good because internally we're still justi-
fying our behavior and blaming others for it.

As you look over your Eighth-Step list, you will realize
that some amends you make can be immediate. If you owe
people money, now is the time to pay it. If you owe a
person so many favors, you've taken advantage of them,
now is the time to return those favors. It is time to
apologize for many of the things you've said or done
which have harmed family, friends and co-workers.

How To Make An Amend

In order to make an amend, you need to . . .

- Completely accept and forgive yourself.
- Completely accept and forgive the other person.
- Fully own responsibility for the harm you have done.
- Be willing to correct the wrong you did.
- Resolve not to repeat it.

Often it helps to practice by writing out a short and
simple apology before you make your amends face to face.
In most cases, saying something like, "I feel regret about
the time I _____ and I want to apologize to
you for that. If there's any way I can correct the situation
between us let me know what I can do," is enough. Sometimes you won't be able to apologize in person. Then
you'll need to write a short note.

You may want to start your amends with one or two
people and situations which have only a small emotional
charge, rather than those with whom you are extremely
close or in situations where you've caused major damage.
In this way you gain practice in being assertive and learning to say what you mean. Be careful, though, not to stay
so long in the practice phase that you procrastinate and
fail to complete the necessary work.

If in the past you typically used, "I'm sorry," as a response to everything and now it has a hollow ring from
overuse and misuse, it is a good idea to avoid it and
discover a new way to phrase your apology. Regret, remorse, guilt, troubled conscience — all serve to jog us out

of the habit of automatically spouting words which have lost their meaning for us.

Whether you speak your amends or write them, make sure you own your feelings and take responsibility for what you did. Don't tell the other person how they must have felt when you harmed them and don't go into lengthy (or even short) rationalizations about why you did what you did. Long complicated apologies only dilute the impact of their content.

Empty form and lengthy explanations are tempting when we approach Step Nine before we've forgiven and accepted ourselves. We're reluctant to place our self-esteem in the hands of others. If someone won't accept our apology, then we find it difficult to move on. We become so stuck in winning their approval, we fail to realize their reluctance to forgive is more of a stumbling block to their growth than to ours. At bottom, the only One who can absolve us from our guilt is our Higher Power. When we've made the effort to apologize and have been rejected, we need to give the problem over to our Higher Power and move on with the business of living sure that we've done all we can.

Don't beg for forgiveness, becoming so emotional that you lay responsibility on the person with whom you are making an amend to erase your guilt. If your amend is a thinly disguised fishing expedition for reassurance, your insincerity will show through and your half-hearted attempt will backfire. Those you make amends to don't owe you anything, not friendship or compassion or understanding. Your hidden expectations for those responses block your healing process by setting you up for failure. People have a way of growing extremely irritated when they feel they're being manipulated and led to feel guilty for harm *we've* done to them — and who can blame them for that? When we demand absolution from others as a condition of our amends, we are, in effect, forcing them to make the amends for us.

Acceptance and forgiveness of others is as much a prerequisite of making amends as acceptance and forgiveness of ourselves. When we harbor grudges against those we've harmed, our Ninth Step is an empty ritual. Even though we may verbally admit to others that we've harmed them and ask that they accept our apology, as long as we hold bitterness against them in our hearts, our words are meaningless.

Fully making amends may take months or even years to complete. It certainly isn't something that can be accomplished in a day or even a week. The important thing is to accomplish as much as you can when you are able to do it, using your list from Step Eight as a tool to periodically review and cut down to size.

Making Amends To Ourselves

We aren't finished with Step Nine until we make amends to ourselves. Again, this is a two-phase process, involving both intention and action. If you've harmed your health and appearance by overeating during your emotionally abusive relationship, now is the time to forgive and accept yourself and start doing something about the self-destructive behavior, be it cutting out desserts or going to an Overeaters Anonymous Group. If you've hurt yourself by sabotaging yourself at work, now you can apologize to the inner you, taking new steps to set career goals and meet them. If you've isolated yourself, forgive yourself and make an effort, to go out and meet people.

Farmers have a saying: *You can't plough a straight furrow looking backward.* The ploughman who looks over his shoulder weaves and wobbles in his progress. As we make amends we release our need to look behind us at the past. We can concentrate on the here and now and move in a straight direction toward where we want to be going. As we let go of our remorse and regrets we move faster to our goal of healing.

In addition the Ninth Step helps build our courage and allows us to see that our feelings aren't totally hooked to the emotions of others. We can forgive ourselves and go on with life, no matter whether the people we've injured forgive us or not. The fact that we make amends doesn't give us control over the reactions of others. When we make amends, we have no guarantee over the outcome. People may accept our apologies or reject them. Relationships may be healed or they may be beyond repair. We learn to accept that no matter which way things go, the most important thing is that we have a right relationship with ourselves and a right relationship with our Higher Power. To achieve this we must clean our lives of shame and guilt and the destructive behaviors we adopted.

Once we have learned from our errors and have taken concrete steps to manifest that new knowledge in the way we relate to others, we release ourselves from the burden of carrying our guilt. When we've made amends, our discomfort no longer serves the purpose of pushing us to right our wrongs. In fact, it serves no purpose whatsoever. We are freed from feeling it and we are freed from the compulsion to constantly repeat our old ways of relating to hide from our shame. In resolving to incorporate the painful lessons of the past into our present lives, we cause them to lose their sting. We are empowered to move forward, no longer hobbled to the point of paralysis by our regrets.

Making amends is a process, and it is the process, not the outcome, which is critical to our healing. When we are squared away with our own consciences and with our Higher Power, our actions flow from a place of serenity and balance.

> *All that I say and all that I do is a testimony to my relationship with myself and with my Higher Power. I accept and forgive myself as I make my amends to those I have harmed.*

13

❧

Step Ten

We continued to take personal inventory and when
we were wrong, promptly admitted it.

*"To be conscious of serious danger and
to be ready to look it in the eye is not pessimism.
It is the way one gathers one's strength.
For when one looks it in the eye, it
becomes interestingly enough, less ominous."*

Dorothy Thompson

The process of self-healing we began when we started
the Twelve-Step Program is a continuous one. If we are to
keep growing, our forward motion doesn't halt next Tues-
day or next Christmas or even five years from today. We
will stretch and transform and overcome throughout the
remaining time we have on this earth. Our self-discovery
and struggles are what keep us emotionally alive and
moving. They provide a fertile field for deep friendships
with others on the healing journey and they keep us in
touch with who we are inside.

No matter how far along we are in our healing, there are times when we'll regress rather than progress. We need to be aware of what we're doing, catch ourselves quickly and immediately get back on course by reworking the steps, paying special attention to Step Four, the inventory. Because learning curves are rarely smooth, our progress is marked by ups and downs, by spirals and plateaus. We need to recognize them when they occur and work to insure that they're only temporary setbacks rather than permanent conditions.

Sometimes getting in touch with our inner anguish carried over from childhood and previous relationships may cause us so much discomfort, we decide to go back to our old ways and shut the door on feeling and vulnerability. At other times, we get caught up in the romance of a new relationship and find co-dependency patterns, once again, taking over our lives. We may grow tired, discouraged and disappointed. When these things happen, rather than beating ourselves up, we can always take another inventory to see where we stand and work from there.

Often when we repeat our inventory we're surprised and pleased with the progress we've already made, the progress we tend to deny or minimize when we're down on ourselves. Our steps toward growth, no matter how small are a significant and solid base on which to build further growth.

New Issues

Quite frequently we find that just when we meet one of our inner challenges, another one comes down the road to confront us. We "beat" our food addiction, our drinking problem or our lack of assertiveness, only to find that we must now struggle with a particularly knotty relationship problem. We conquer our relationship problem, then realize that we have no goals in life. We've been aimlessly drifting in terms of work. We go back to school and set career goals, then we discover major tears in the fabric of our relationships with our children. Stripping away one layer of faults and wrongs reveals yet another, deeper layer.

As the external circumstances of our lives change, we face new sets of issues, too, some of which we never knew existed. We receive a promotion and must tackle our fear of success and tendency to self-sabotage. We have a baby and need to learn how to be a parent who will not pass on the legacy of co-dependency. A child leaves home and strikes out into the world and we have to sort through a set of abandonment issues and feelings, similar to, but not quite the same as, the ones we faced with our emotionally abusive partners. Relationships end. Relationships begin. We substitute old worn-out life goals for new ones.

As each new issue surfaces and with each change of circumstances, our tendency may be to ignore the challenge that is presented to us. We want to hide or to take a vacation from the difficult work of becoming the whole and healthy people we were meant to be. Sometimes, too, we may feel stuck, wanting to move on, but not knowing where to begin. When we ignore our challenges, refusing to look them in the eye, they grow into dangerous pitfalls. Acknowledging and embracing our challenges cuts them down to size.

The inventory step is a touchstone that is always there for us, a way for us to access and assess our inner resources. The task of nurturing our strengths and releasing our weaknesses, of finding and maintaining our balance, then moving out into the world to practice what we've learned is as vital to our existence as breathing.

After we've grown adept at inventory and have incorporated it as a natural and essential part of our lives, we can begin to use the procedure as a tool, creatively mining ourselves for information about who we are and how we can live up to our highest potentials. Because each one of us uses different energy patterns to store memories, each one of us needs to access that material in our inner selves differently. For some of us making lists helps. Others work better drawing pictures, talking into a tape recorder or dancing or acting out a memory. We may write poetry or keep a journal. Since our experiences, our personalities and our learning styles differ, so do our methods of looking inward.

The key to continued advanced inventory and growth is to learn to listen to your inner voice, to act on the guidance it brings. Invent your own exercises for self-discovery. Talk with a therapist or a good friend in order to generate new insights and check out the old ones. If you've never been involved with groups before but an Adult Children of Dysfunctional Families or a Co-dependents Anonymous group sounds interesting, go for it. If you find yourself attracted to a workshop or a lecture, attend. When a book title piques your interest, read it. Should a wilderness therapy trip come your way and you want to go, then go! The input we receive from these experiences not only recharges our batteries, it often causes us to look inward and re-inventory based on the new information and perceptions we've absorbed.

As we become seekers, we constantly need to ask ourselves — Does this new information feel right to me? Does it fit with my life? Can it work? Will it further the kind of person I want to be?

Those questions are a further inventory, moving us along the path toward self-knowledge as we learn to set limits, rejecting opinions and techniques which are harmful to our recovery. They also help us develop an internal sense of honesty and move away from co-dependency toward self-empowerment. The only one who can give us the answers to who we are is ourselves.

In time inventory becomes a daily process we practice without conscious intent. As naturally as we ride a bicycle or drive a car, we automatically check our inner and outer reality and make the necessary adjustments. We no longer need to sit down with pen and paper because we are in a state of mindfulness most of the time. In the meantime, exercises such as the ones which follow, can help us get to that place.

Relationship Graphs

Making a relationship graph gives a visual picture of the highs and lows of your connections with other people and helps to bring up repressed information, essential for self-awareness. These graphs also depict patterns in our love lives, throwing our repetition compulsions into sharp focus and pointing the way toward positive change.

Start by drawing a long, horizontal, straight line on a large piece of paper. This line represents your life. Divide the line into segments. These can represent individual years or two, three or five year chunks of time, whichever works best for you. Starting from the beginning of your awareness, think about the predominant relationship you had with your mother in each segment of your past. Represent each relationship by drawing a dot either above or below the line. Dots above the baseline will stand for positive relationships, the higher the dot, the more positive the relationship. The further below the line you place the dots, the more negative feelings you carry about the events or feelings the dot symbolizes. Label the dots with a short note to yourself about why you placed the dot where you did. Connect the dots.

Now, using a different colored pen or pencil go through the same process to draw your continuing relationship with your father. Next, using a new color, graph your relationships with men, charting the highs and lows. Finally, plot points which symbolize how you felt about yourself, carefully drawing dots to show your periods of high, low and average self-esteem.

Your life relationships graph might look something like this:

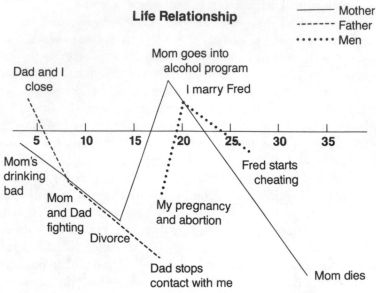

Life Relationship

—— Mother
------ Father
•••••• Men

Dad and I close

Mom goes into alcohol program

I marry Fred

5   10   15   20   25   30   35

Mom's drinking bad

Mom and Dad fighting

Divorce

Fred starts cheating

My pregnancy and abortion

Dad stops contact with me

Mom dies

Study the graph to become more aware of both the direction and the interplay of relationships in your past. Have your relationships with your mother and with your father stayed stable or have they changed over the years? Have they improved or grown more negative? When the relationship with your father was negative, was there a compensatory positive relationship with your mother and vice versa? Or was your relationship with your parents uniformly good or bad from your perspective?

Look at the line you've used to represent your relationships with men. Have those relationships started high and been going downhill ever since? Or did they start out being very negative, improving one relationship at a time? You may find that you've experienced very little change over the years, that your male/female relationships have been uniformly negative. Compare your male/female relationships line with the lines you've drawn for parents. When the man/woman relationship line is high, where do the parent points stand? We may use love relationships to isolate ourselves from our parents or to run from a troubled family situation.

By scanning our charts, we can start to determine whether we've repeated the same old dysfunctional relationships over and over again, simply substituting new people for old or using our relationships with men as stepping-stones from which to change and grow. We can also get some indication of whether we're unrealistically loyal or run from others rather than working through conflicts. We can start to get a sense of how much we act and how much we allow ourselves to be acted upon. Does trouble with a parent seem to trigger trouble with a spouse or lover or is the reverse true? When we notice periods of time when all of our relationships were negative except for one, we may have been expecting that one person to meet all our needs.

The interplay and complexity of our relationships to others is ever-changing. When we detect patterns in those changes, we can stop trying to control others. True intimacy then becomes possible for us.

An interesting and useful way to carry this exercise a step further is to graph the course of our individual love relationships, starting with our current one or the one we just ended. Use a separate piece of typing paper for each relationship and again draw dots representing positive and negative events chronologically, above and below the time line.

A sample graph might look like this:

Love Relationship

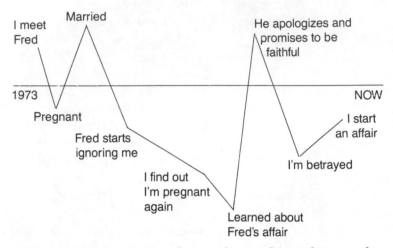

Once you've completed your love relationship graphs, look them over for patterns. Even though you may have loved some very different types of men, the characteristics of your relationships with them may have been remarkably the same. Do the relationships start off at a low point and then peak when your urge to rescue and mother takes over? Do the high points come before or after major crises? How long has it taken you to cycle through relationships? Often by visually comparing the "look" of our past relationships, we can begin to pick up on their fatal flaws.

If we keep repeating the same old relationship with different love objects, we can begin to sort out just what went wrong and how much of it had to do with our behaviors — from picking an immature emotionally abusive man to mothering him or reinforcing his negative and destructive behaviors. Part of the inventory process is to figure out what *we* did wrong and step beyond focusing on how the men in our lives did us wrong. Forewarned is forearmed. Once we understand our tendencies, we are able to avoid the traps we lay for our lovers and for ourselves.

The Art Of Inner Exploration

Often today we hide our latent artistic talents from ourselves because when we were kids, we were told that trees aren't purple and cows aren't green. Artistic expression became a way of people-pleasing we may have grudgingly resented. Yet art can be a very powerful tool for accessing our emotions since we store so many of them in our bodies. Art is a very kinesthetic tactile way of opening up the flow.

Begin collecting art supplies. You might want an inexpensive set of finger paints and some felt-tip markers. If you always coveted the big box of crayons with the sharpener in the back, now is the time to buy it for yourself. Give yourself permission to let your tools be your own. Do not lend them to others. It's a good idea, too, to work on your initial art projects in private. We're often so used to censoring ourselves because of what others might think, that even doing this type of work in the presence of our young children is constricting. The object is to have fun, let yourself go and learn about your interior pictures.

The suggestions below offer some starting points.

- Draw a full-body portrait of yourself and next to it a likeness of the man you are currently involved with or your most current partner in a long-term relationship. When you've finished, analyze the picture for clues about your relationship. How close or distant are you? How is he dressed compared to the way you're dressed? What are the expressions on your faces? Which of his body parts did you emphasize or de-emphasize, either by size or detail? Which of yours are emphasized and de-emphasized? What do you think the picture says about your relationship to each other and your priorities? Does it point to some hidden issues you may want to work on?

- Generate further insights by drawing or painting family pictures of your family of origin and asking yourself the same questions you did about your love relationship picture. Try a series of family portraits, starting when you were born and adding siblings as they were born. When you've completed your project, compare the pictures. What similarities and differences do you notice? Who looks the most powerful? Who looks the most powerless? Are your figures placed far apart or are they clumped close together? What do the portraits tell you about your family history?

- Collect old magazines and try making a collage of yourself. Limit yourself to using various inanimate objects for your features. When you finish, analyze the picture to learn more about how you view yourself. What did you use for eyes? What did you use for ears? What about hands, arms and legs? What do you think your picture is trying to tell you about your self-esteem and how you operate in the world?

- Native Americans from many tribes used medicine shields as a form of psychic protection and affirmation. Draw a circle on paper and then choose power symbols to place inside. These symbols can either stand for what you feel are your strong points or for qualities you desire to develop within. Hang your medicine shield in a place where you will see it often and be reminded of your intent to be strong.

- When you're feeling a particularly potent emotion and having difficulty dealing with it, try to fingerpaint it, using the colors and movements you feel best capture exactly what it is you're experiencing. Go with what you're feeling as much as you can. When you finish, give your picture a different, more creative title than the emotion itself. What does the title say about what you're feeling? Now try on another sheet of paper, fingerpainting the emotion you wish you could be feeling.

- Try sculpting a self-portrait or representations of your feelings in pottery clay, available in five-pound boxes in art stores. If you've never worked with clay, this can be a powerful way to get in touch with repressed emotions and experiences. You might want to move on to sculpting your family of origin, your children and your partner, in order to discover how you feel about them and the relationships you have with them.

Journal Writing

Many of us have the same blocks against writing down our feelings as we do about drawing or painting them. Either we feel as if we were back in school and must turn in a "perfect" composition in order to please a teacher or else we tell ourselves we have nothing worth saying. Yet when we learn to free-write and stop our self-censorship, we often come to amazing insights about ourselves. Therapeutic journal writing isn't the same as the old five-year diaries we used to get for Christmas and kept up only until mid-January. Journals can serve as a good way to assess the changes we're making and those we need to make. They are a record of our thoughts and feelings, rather than a record of the relatively minor events which make up many of our days.

Before you begin your journal writing, find a book and a pen which please you. Some women like bound blank books with fancy fabric or leather covers. Others feel more comfortable with steno pads or black cardboard-covered composition books. Legal pads work, too. Some of us prefer writing with pencils and others wouldn't be caught without our favorite felt-tip pen. Experiment in order to discover what feels best to you.

Pick a time when you are relaxed and a place where you can be alone and free from distractions. If writing comes easily to you, then go ahead and do it. If you, like so many of us, have a phobia about blank pages, you might want to use one of the following suggestions to get you started. Some you may do only once or choose not to try at all. Others may prove to be very useful to you and you'll feel drawn to do them several times. It is critical to write

whatever comes into your mind, not worrying about pen-
manship or grammar. Your journal is a record of your
inner journey and for your eyes only unless you choose to
share parts of it with others.

- Think back to your earliest memory and write about
  it, recalling the smells, sounds, tastes, textures and
  sights. What colors did you see? What emotions did
  you feel?

- Graph your school years, year-by-year, as you did
  with your relationships. Now pick the highest high or
  the lowest low and try to capture it with words, including as much vivid sensory and emotional detail
  as you can.

- Make a list of your life's milestones, the turning
  points you regard as important measures of your
  progress. Pick one and write about it in the present
  tense as if you were reliving it now. When you finish
  describing the milestone, write about why it was/is so
  important to you.

- Write a biography, starting with your earliest memory
  and continuing to the present day. As you write,
  focus on the people, places, events, and feelings which
  were important to you, not those you think should be
  important. (Often we find that marriages, college
  degrees or even winning the lottery pale emotionally
  compared to events like our first period, the time we
  learned to ride a two-wheeled bike or the day we
  decided to lose ten pounds.)

- Think about the favorite part of your body and the
  least favorite part of your body. If you've never
  thought about your body, you may need to stand in
  front of a full-length mirror to decide. Now write
  letters to both of them, telling them exactly how you
  feel and why. When you've finished, allow those parts
  of your body to write back to you, telling what they
  want from you and what you can do for them, so
  they'll be happier. (If you suffer from headaches or

muscle tension, writing to the area of your body which hurts can be a good way of getting to the psychological source of pain.)

- All of us carry an inner child inside, the hurt, scared, angry part of ourselves which often takes control of our emotions and actions as adults when we deny or ignore her. Write a series of letters to her about troublesome events in your life today and allow her to write replies. Ask your interior little girl how she feels and what she needs you to do for her.

- Dialogue with your emotions. Whenever you're feeling strongly pulled by something you don't want to feel, picture it as a character. For instance, your sadness might be an elderly stooped bag lady with grey and wrinkled skin. Your pain might be a hairy little demon with glowing eyes and a pitchfork. The more vivid your characterization, the more effective this exercise will be. Now write a biographical sketch of your emotion. When and where was it born? What was its childhood like? What was it doing five years ago? What are its likes and dislikes? When you have a clear picture of your emotion, write a dialogue with it, asking it the questions you want answered and giving it free rein when it replies.

- Once you have several emotions fully characterized, you might want to write a fable or fairy tale using them as the main characters. When you've finished, read your story over and see if it has any parallels to your exterior life and if there is anything you can learn from the tale. What's the moral to the story? Some of the cast of characters you might want to work with are . . . envy, jealousy, grief, loneliness, anger, fear, anxiety, depression, joy, serenity and love.

- Trying using your characters in a love story.

- Our lives can be a confusing mix of opposites at times. Often we feel a great deal of tension centering around polarized qualities. One big one for us is dependence

versus independence. Another is generosity versus
being able to take. Make a list of the opposites which
hold the most charge for you and try to describe each
extreme. As you write, focus on the good and bad
characteristics for each end of the spectrum.

- Pick a quality you'd like to develop more in yourself
and write everything that comes to your mind about
that quality. If it were a color, what color would it be?
If it had a taste, what would it taste like? How would
it feel if you could hold it in your hand? What sort of
sound does it make? What aroma does it give off?
What does it remind you of from your past experience or your life today? When you've finished writing about your quality, ask it what you need to do in
order to entice it into your life. Write down the reply.
Some qualities you might want to work with in this
manner are . . .

Simplicity	Balance	Calmness
Love	Compassion	Tenderness
Forgiveness	Acceptance	Healing
Responsibility	Efficiency	Power
Integrity	Patience	Persistence
Understanding	Wisdom	Clarity
Curiosity	Honesty	Trust
Logic	Openness	Intimacy
Sensuality	Willingness	Release
Independence	Gratitude	Harmony
Purpose	Faith	Optimism
Creativity	Spontaneity	Delight
Wonder	Playfulness	Humor
Adventure	Enthusiasm	Flexibility
Strength	Abundance	Spirituality

- Start a journal entry with "I am the kind of person
who . . ." and write down the concrete characteristics
you feel best define you at present. When you get
stuck, repeat the opening phrase. (Developing this
sort of rhythm almost to the point of chant in your

writing can help unstick ideas and get you to be more fluent with your thoughts.) Now, pretend you're living five years into the future and repeat the exercise from that perspective. When you're done, compare the two pieces of writing to note the ways in which you'd like to change.

The better we know ourselves, the easier it is to be true to the purpose our Higher Power has in mind for us. When we do wrong to others and to ourselves, we can immediately be willing to have our shortcomings removed and to ask God to remove them, then make amends to the people we've hurt, including ourselves.

Theoretically, if we did no wrong, we could be assured of living guilt-free lives. Because we are human and incapable of ever being perfect, that option is an impossible one. To think we can fix ourselves and go on to live flawlessly is to be caught in grandiosity, delusion and denial — dangerous traps to our recovery.

What we *can* do is to periodically examine our interior landscape and purify ourselves from the guilt and shame we carry. Step Ten frees us to live to our highest potential today and tomorrow and all the tomorrows we have in store.

My inward journey is the most exciting and necessary adventure I will ever undertake. I approach this task with the serenity to accept what I cannot change about myself, the courage to change what I can, and the wisdom to know the difference.

14

※

Step Eleven

We sought through prayer and meditation to improve
our conscious contact with God as
we understood God, praying only for knowledge
of God's will for us and the power
to carry that out.

"This sentence expresses my theology
in a few words: 'It is enough to know that
God's responsibility is irrevocable, and
His resources limitless.' "

Hannah Whitall Smith

Step Eleven encourages us to build on the relationship
we've already begun to establish with our Higher Power,
expanding our spiritual development a step further into
the realm of the irrevocable responsibility and limitless
resources of God. When we improve our conscious contact with our Higher Power, that means we're doing
nothing more esoteric and complex than deliberately and

actively improving our communication. We do this in two ways: through prayer or talking to God/Goddess and through meditation or listening to Mother/Father God. Our Higher Power is always there for us, ready to listen and ready to help us live our lives if only we are willing to ask for direction and be receptive to taking it.

We are cautioned in Step Eleven only to ask for knowledge of our Higher Power's will and the strength and energy to carry that will out. In these times when much willful and materialistic teaching abounds, which views the Higher Power as a Santa Claus wearing the disguise of many traditions from Zen to traditional Christianity, this caution takes on special significance. It is not our place to determine that what we need to make us happy is a new man or a Mercedes-Benz, then ask God for those things as if we were placing our order with a divine mail order business, as some would urge us to do. Neither is it our place to petition our Higher Power to save our marriage, get us a job with a particular company or help our children earn scholarships to Harvard. We need to ask only to know the Divine's will and for the courage, patience and persistence to act on that, rather than our own head-strong impulses, mindful that it was our own willfulness which helped us create unmanageable lives to begin with.

A second important aspect of the Eleventh Step is that it focuses on our relationship to God/dess as *we* know Him/Her. That personal knowledge is critical if we are to avoid the ever-present temptation to become enmeshed with a sect or doctrine which has all the elements of an emotionally abusive relationship. Our upbringing and past relationships make these groups very attractive and comfortable on the surface, but when we attach ourselves to a group which controls through psychological violence, coercion or manipulation, we too often fall into our familiar roles as victims. We allow other group members to batter our self-esteem and hold the organization-sanctioned beliefs above our personal relationship with our Higher Power. We stop thinking and feeling for ourselves and mistrust our perceptions, sliding back into co-dependency. Eventually we begin living on the outside again, avoiding the inner life we sought in the first place.

How To Hear Our Higher Power

That private and contemplative inner life is essential if we are to cultivate a deep and rewarding relationship with the All That Is. Before we can retreat to the quiet place inside ourselves and make contact with our Higher Power, we must learn to develop an internal spiritual life, rather than an external one more dependent on others than on our Higher Power. No matter how outwardly directed our lives have become, there are ways in which we can nurture ourselves so that we have the time, energy and inclination to find the serenity and the voice of God that is within each one of us, waiting for us to discover it.

Privacy and solitude are very important for developing contact with our Higher Power. How can we tune into the still, small voice when all around us we hear babble and hubbub? If, by a miracle, we should hear the voice of our Higher Power amid the static of our overly frantic lives, how could we give the message any consideration in the turmoil of our day-to-day existence? Often without thinking, we allow our lives to become a frantic cluttered endurance contest, and in order to grow spiritually, we must start to reclaim time and space for ourselves.

When we set out to talk with God and to listen, it is essential to find a place where we can be alone. The space we choose for prayer and meditation need not be elaborate. A bedroom with a Do-Not-Disturb sign, the bathroom when we take our evening bath, the kitchen table when everyone is away — all work equally well. If we can't find the space we need for solitude at home, we can develop the habit of taking an evening walk or popping into an unlocked church sanctuary during our lunch break.

We also need to make time in our daily routine for prayer and meditation. While grabbing moments catch as catch can to talk with and listen to our Higher Power is

better than nothing, for real spiritual growth
in our lives, we need to make it a priority.
devoting a regular piece of time to our spirit
daily basis. Whether we set the alarm for 15 min
each morning or cut back on the chores we feel
perform, scheduling regular times to commune
Higher Power is a living affirmation of our intent to
our spirituality a top priority in our lives.

When we tell ourselves that we can't possibly ma
time or find a place to be alone for a relationship with
Higher Power, we need to rethink our priorities. Once
establish a good Higher Power relationship, we often
we have more time than we did before, because we're
longer going around in circles. Even though taking tim
for ourselves may feel selfish to us at the beginning an
may certainly seem selfish to those around us who are
used to having us put their needs first, it is critical to our
healing. Times of solitude and spiritual grounding are
essential to our survival. We have very little to give others
when we haven't learned to emotionally nourish ourselves
and learned to allow our Higher Power to nurture us.

The old saying, *"The Lord helps those who help themselves,"*
couldn't be more true. Until we help ourselves to spiritual
time, we are shutting the door on communication with the
Higher Power and closing out the possibility of a serene
and rewarding life.

Our Physical Bodies

How we care for our physical bodies can be a critical
factor in our spirituality as well. When we're run down,
stuffed with doughnuts, hyped with caffeine and panting
from too many cigarettes, we aren't living in harmony or
accord with the best we can be — the people our Higher
Power has created us to be. The quiet self-discipline of
prayer and meditation are difficult because we have trouble concentrating and we're too physically exhausted to
carry out our Higher Power's will for our lives. The
Judeo-Christian tradition teaches that our bodies are the
temples of our souls. Many other religious teachings also

place emphasis on moderation in physical habits as a key to increased spiritual as well as physical health.

As we honestly look at our excesses and do something about them, we need to ask ourselves . . . Do we drink too much? Have we become dependent on cigarettes? Do we take too many prescription drugs to deal with stress? Are we substituting food for the love and affection we're unwilling to give to ourselves? Drugs, alcohol, tobacco, food and even sex can be used as mood alterers. We become distanced from our feelings, even though we may fool ourselves into believing that we're really in touch with them or even with the Divine. Some of us may have come to view eating or drinking or drugging as religious experiences in and of themselves because they alter our moods and in some ways mimic states of higher consciousness. If we suspect we're dependent on some substance, that it has become our god, we need to seek therapy or get involved with a Twelve-Step group to help us deal with our addiction as a prerequisite for improving our conscious contact with God/dess.

As we look at the way we treat our bodies, we may discover deficiencies rather than excesses. Perhaps we don't exercise or we eat very little nutritious food. In fact, we might eat very little food at all — to the point of becoming anorexic. Maybe we dress in dumpy and uncomfortable clothing and fail to get enough sleep at night so that our eyes are ringed with dark circles. Often we deny our physical needs in an attempt to punish ourselves as a sort of misguided exercise we may even term spiritual. Whether we're starved or simply exhausted, our mistreatment of our bodies prevents us from having a relationship with the Divine. When we *do* get glimmers of our Higher Power's plan for us, we're too addicted to self-denial to carry it out!

Our Protective Boundaries

Just as we need to take time and space for solitude and take care of our physical selves, we must respect ourselves enough to enforce our boundaries if we are to grow in a spiritual direction.

When our children wait until the last minute to tell us, then expect us to stay up all night to sew costumes for them, we need to say no.

When a verbally abusive spouse becomes threatened by our diet and teases us, then tempts us with candy as a ploy to get us to regain weight, we need to say no.

Our boundaries are how we define our personal integrity. When we set reasonable boundaries and stick to them, we are exercising self-respect. Without self-respect we cannot respect a Power outside ourselves. In the case of knowing our physical limits and living within them, we're telling ourselves and, in effect, the world that we have enough self-esteem to want to be healthy and stick around the planet for a while, that we're confident our Higher Power has plans for us, and we want to be able to carry them out.

Simplify

Sometimes we need to go beyond setting limits on our time, space, energy and physical well-being. We must look around us at the material and emotional clutter in our lives. We may find our home filled with useless possessions we care little or nothing for, yet we remain tied to them — afraid to leave home because somebody might break in, dusting instead of spending time in other more growth-promoting and productive ways. Our days may be crammed with people and pastimes we've outgrown as well. We obsess over how a neighbor from 12 years ago, a neighbor we never really liked, will feel if we don't send her a birthday card. We spend our nights watching TV shows we can't stand out of force of habit, then claim we never have time to do the things we want to do.

The clutter of possessions, of people and of activities in our lives, turns us away from the spiritual path. Seekers over the centuries have known that to move closer to God requires not only a temporary retreat but a gradual and permanent moving away from some of life's attachments and distractions. Simplifying our lives insures we have the time and the proper attitude to hear what our Higher Power has to tell us. We're not so caught up in the physical and material realities of our lives that we can ignore the spiritual.

We can begin to simplify by being mindful of our possessions, our commitments to people and the ways we spend our time, asking ourselves just how much we need to have yet another thing. We need to question whether or not a particular person, purchase or pastime is energy depleting or energy enhancing. The less complex our lifestyles, the easier it is for us to find the time and money for enriching experiences we never dreamed were available to us before, like further education or travel. We may find that all the tiny household gods we've erected in our lives are keeping us from setting goals, thinking clearly and from connecting with our God/dess and doing His or Her will. When we clean the clutter from our lives, we also clear the distraction from our minds so that we can become an open channel for spirit guided life.

We can also learn to fill ourselves and our lives with positive, uplifting experiences. Computer programmers have a saying, "Garbage in, garbage out." It works that way in the rest of the world, too. The more beauty and wisdom we incorporate into our lives, the closer we put ourselves in touch with nature, the more beautiful, true and natural our actions become. We can make it a point to actively seek to feed ourselves spiritually by reading inspirational material, interacting with people we feel are further along the spiritual path than we and by directly experiencing the world our Creator has provided for us.

Be Expectant

Another way we open ourselves to God is by generating a feeling of expectancy, faith that our Higher Power will listen to us and faith that our Higher Power will speak to us. Understanding and forgiving ourselves is a prerequisite to joyfully expectant faith. We need to realize that when we put ourselves down, we're really insulting our

Higher Power because we are presumably made in that Higher Power's image. Our self-understanding and acceptance, unconditional love, is a form of nurturing that's necessary in our relationship with our God. When we hold ourselves in such low regard that we feel unworthy to ask the Divine for assistance or to hear what God has to say to us, we allow pessimism and lack of faith to exile us from any hope of spiritual life.

Ironically this pseudohumility is actually a form of self-pity which is egotism and grandiosity in disguise. When we say we believe we're not worthy of our Higher Power's love or understanding, we're actually saying that we can live without guidance from the Divine — it's not our fault; it's our Higher Power's. We "know" that our Higher Power would reject us if we tried to form a close relationship, therefore, we'll do the rejecting first, cut our losses and save ourselves some pain. When we assume this stance, what we're attempting is to be little gods ourselves, to control God and manipulate the Divine into taking pity on us because we're no good. It is the same self-serving posture many of us adopted during the course of our abusive relationships. It didn't work then and it won't work now.

We are told in the Bible to love our neighbors *as we love ourselves.* That strongly implies that God requires us to have some degree of self-esteem. Psychologists, too, insist that healthy self-love is at the base of all good relationships — so it stands to reason this is true even of the one with our Creator. The key to developing a conscious contact with our Higher Power is the core belief that we are worthy of the Divine's protection, attention and affection.

Another form of nurturing is going after what we need without feeling guilty about it and stopping ourselves. When we open ourselves to our Higher Power's plan for our lives and then don't carry it out, we're only going halfway in our spiritual lives. When we listen very carefully to our Higher Power, we are certain of our needs. We may discover we need to form a friendship outside of our home or need to take a workshop in relaxation techniques. Even though it may not make a great deal of sense to our rational minds, our Higher Power is constantly revealing to us just what it is we need to do next and pointing our steps in that direction.

When we struggle against the guidance from the Divine, we usually use the weapons of doubt and guilt, telling ourselves we must be crazy going back to school at our age or that if we even took one class, our families couldn't survive without us. So we stop ourselves from doing what we need to do, what our Higher Power tells us we must do in order to fulfill ourselves. While it's too scary to openly defy Divine wisdom, it is much safer and easier to convince ourselves and our Higher Power that we can't put His or Her plan for us into action. It sounds so much better than saying we won't obey orders from above. Our helplessness may hide our willfulness and lack of obedience from ourselves, but our Higher Power isn't fooled by our deception.

In order to expand our spiritual life, we must be prepared to act on the wisdom that the All That Is reveals to us. That means being a good listener, remaining flexible and nonjudgmental enough to hear what's actually being said to us without twisting the message to fit with the preconceived filters through which we view life. It also means being open to being stretched and pushed into new situations which will accelerate our growth at a faster pace than we may feel entirely comfortable with. When we have stage fright, our Higher Power may push us in the direction of public speaking about emotionally abusive relationships. We can refuse and stagnate . . . or we can risk taking a leap of faith and grow. Our Higher Power never gives us more than we can handle and never pushes us in directions in which it is not right for us to move.

Seeking Spiritual Wisdom

There are times when we may feel we need the help of a teacher or a spiritual advisor. Whether we read books or take classes in Christian meditation or we sign up for yoga workshops, the more spiritual techniques or practices we expose ourselves to, the better we are able to choose what works most effectively to foster *our* relationship with the Divine. Although the Medieval Christian tradition was steeped in meditation techniques, for years the emphasis on listening to God, rather than only petitioning God, was lost. Today many traditional Christian faiths, both Protestant and Catholic, are looking to Eastern techniques in order to realign themselves with the technique of quiet listening for the voice of God to speak in our lives. Abundant resources are available.

You might want to seek out a meditation teacher, to explore the sitting of zazen or the meditative movements of sacred dance. It is important to follow the path where it takes you without guilt or a can't-do attitude. It is also important to understand that we generally attract the types of teachers to us whom we need at the moment. When we suspect a person we've chosen to learn from is hypocritical or a materialistic charlatan, that can be a learning experience, too. We learn how to set spiritual boundaries and to assertively enforce them. When we enter into the study of spirituality with an open mind and with an open heart, we soon become aware that we can't buy enlightenment for any price.

Wherever you seek spiritual wisdom, whether from a minister or a teacher, the voice of the Divine inside of you should be your ultimate guide. When you encounter a set of teachings or a new practice, ask yourself how it feels to you? Is it harmonious with your growing sense of the Divine or is it discordant? Does the practice require you to do things you hold against your moral and ethical values? Is this teaching a positive or negative force in your life? Learn to rely on your Higher Power for guidance in seeking guidance.

In time and with practice we find that we can hear the voice of our Higher Power inside of us more clearly and receive Divine guidance on all sorts of issues from the major decisions to the minor day-to-day hassles. At times we may fear, we're deceiving ourselves or that we're irrational. All we need to do is listen and be honest about sorting our Higher Power's urgings from those of our own ego. Just as we pray from the deepest place within our hearts, we need to learn to listen with our hearts, quieting the chatter or ego in our heads and allowing wisdom to flow through us unimpeded by selfish desires and fears. Our Higher Power's will for our actions is never destructive or negative in tone or in content. At some level we always know what is true and what is false. Our task is to allow ourselves to operate on that level, instead of on the level of self-serving illusion.

Guidance Or Self-Delusion?

One way we can avoid deluding ourselves is by releasing our investment in a specific answer to the guidance question we're posing to our Higher Power. It is important that we seek only the truth, not the predetermined answers we desire to hear the most. Certainly it's fine to share what we want to hear from God with God, but we need to be fully prepared that the answers communicated to us may not be the ones we feel most comfortable hearing. It may simply not be part of the plan for us to ever have a Mercedes or our kids go to Harvard. The Divine knows more about what we really need than we do.

We also need to release concrete expectations about the outcome of our meditation. Some people do claim that merely by asking God, they receive fancy cars, big houses and fur coats. When we listen to their advice, we may feel envious and like failures. Walking in harmony with the All That Is helps to dramatize to us that our Higher Power can provide for all of our needs, but God is not a cosmic Santa Claus or a wish-granting fairy. When we treat the Divine as such, we trivialize our spiritual pursuits. We also fall into the false and materialistic trap of measuring the success of our spiritual quest in terms of our material possessions. We judge ourselves and others based on the exterior trappings they own, the cars, the clothes, the electronic gadgets, rather than by their internal essences. What they wear becomes more important than who they are. The haves must be holy and in touch with the Divine, we think. The have-nots, therefore, must be bad. Such simplistic reasoning drives us even further away from God.

Another expectation we must release early on is that the spiritual results of our prayer and meditation will be the same as those of others on the same or similar paths. The voice of God or the Goddess doesn't speak to everyone in the same way. Even though some people may actually hear messages, others find their answers come in dreams.

The voice of the Divine is everywhere — waiting for us to perceive it. It may come when we pick up a brochure for a weekend retreat and are hit with a sudden and intense "knowing" that we need to attend. The wisdom our Higher Power wants us to learn can be revealed to us through stories or songs or in a worship context. Lessons can also be revealed through positive experiences with friends and loved ones and through some very tough challenges at the hands of those we believe are our enemies. Just as our Higher Power makes certain our nurturance needs are met, He/She makes sure that our growth needs are met. Often that means tossing a particularly sticky challenge our way.

Some people experience flashes of enlightenment when they first begin to meditate and they are disappointed when these dramatic experiences fall off and the experience becomes humdrum. Other people work at meditation for years and years and never experience what they hear others describe as an altered state of consciousness. There are no hard and fast timetables for the results of meditation. It is clear from listening to people who have practiced it for a length of time, that entering the process with an open let's-see attitude which is nonjudgmental and has few specific expectations, will bring the most long-lasting and positive spiritual results.

Finally, in order to see results in our lives, we need to discipline ourselves to stick with our prayer and meditation program. Simply setting aside time, doesn't guarantee we'll want to use it. There will be days we don't feel like taking quiet time to be alone with our Higher Power and days that when we do find the time, our thoughts are so distracted we seem to accomplish nothing during the minutes we spend in prayer and meditation. Overcoming those stumbling blocks is a critical part of the pathway of the inner life. Often we learn more from our resistances than we do from the aspects of the spiritual life which come easiest for us.

We are learning to slow down, to take each moment as it comes and to live in harmony with the Divine. There are no short cuts on this path, but when we begin to follow the core prayer and meditation techniques taught by wise men and women through the centuries and those we discover on our own, we find our consciousness of God and our lives expanded. Truly we are blessed.

I am learning to quiet the inner chatter of my mind in order to hear my Higher Power's guidance for my life, and I pray for the courage, strength and determination to carry it out.

15

Step Twelve

Having had a spiritual awakening as a result of
these steps, we tried to carry this message to others,
and to practice these principles in all our affairs.

*"I avoid looking forward or backward and try to
keep looking upward."*

Charlotte Bronte

The spiritual awakening so important in Step Twelve can
occur in many ways, each different from but not necessarily
better than the others. Some women awaken by gentle
stages, experiencing a dawning consciousness, then drifting
back to the sleep of old patterns for a time before they
revive again, each time rousing further. Others become
conscious at once as if an alarm had gone off. They are
immediately and fully alert, ready to begin the work ahead.

No matter how this awakening unfolds, faithfully following the Twelve Steps undeniably does give us the gift
of a new spiritual awareness. We become conscious of our

inherent unity with all that exists, and the focus of our lives changes from a shortsighted viewpoint fixed on ourselves to an ability to take in the broader picture and to see our place in it.

As we grow completely attuned to the presence of our Higher Power in our lives and willingly allow that Power to direct our actions, the very fabric of our existence changes. Somehow the snags and flaws we dwelled upon as impediments to our fulfillment become opportunities for transcendence. We learn to take the ripped and torn garment of our past and reweave it into a foundation for a beautiful useful life, transforming the conditions we once believed were totally negative into motivation for positive actions.

Our visions are turned toward the blessings in life, creative opportunities for growth and our chances to improve ourselves. No longer at the mercy of our negative and self-defensive thoughts, feelings and actions, we look upward rather than feeling guilty about the past or worrying about the future. Often we find our lives flow more smoothly than we'd ever dreamed possible.

This new ease with which we travel our days is based on working the Twelve-Step Program. If we forget the very real struggles and steps which triggered our awakening, we run the risk of falling asleep again and drifting away from the Twelve Steps. Our growth doesn't stop with the spiritual awakening mentioned in Step Twelve. In fact, it has just begun.

Caring, Not Controlling

Since we've freed a great deal of energy within ourselves, it's only natural to want to expend it, changing what we perceive to be the wrongs in the world around us. As Step Twelve instructs, we need to carry the message to others. In our initial enthusiasm we may mistakenly decide it is within our power to fix our friends, relatives and co-workers. Too often our initial efforts to carry the message backfire, and we're left feeling disappointed and confused — two of the familiar feelings we remember from our emotionally abusive relationships. We've found enlightenment. Now why can't those we know and love just listen to us and do the same?

We need to always keep in mind that attempting to spread the healing message of the Twelve Steps is not the same as zealously winning converts or rescuing others. Making ourselves responsible for their choices snaps us back into our old co-dependency patterns. This time instead of wanting to control our psychological abuser's rage attacks, we wish to manipulate the spiritual development of the people around us. Because we confuse caring about people with taking care of them, we may distort the mandate of Step Twelve's spreading the message to include not only telling others about our recovery and the Twelve Steps, but spoon-feeding this information to them or actually trying to cram it down their throats.

Not everyone shares the same path we do. We can live our lives as examples of the healing power of the Twelve Steps and openly and honestly share the story of our recovery with others, but when we desire to convert others to our way of thinking, we become controlling, turning more people off to the message than we convince.

One of the Twelve Traditions of Alcoholics Anonymous, which has been adopted by many other self-help groups, states that these groups draw others toward them by attraction rather than promotion. In short, if we've had a spiritual awakening and are living our lives accordingly, we, too, will attract others to the path we follow with no need for strong-arm tactics. We do not need to verbally push to convince people that what we're doing works. They can see it in our every action. We do not need to drag them to Twelve Step meetings. Our serenity shines like a beacon pointing the way toward recovery for others.

When we feel compelled to manipulate and coerce others into the program of recovery we've found so beneficial, we need to get back to our Twelve Step basics, acknowledging that we can't control the decisions of others, admitting the dysfunctionality of our pushiness and making amends for it. As we grow more accustomed to the inner tranquility of our spiritual awakening, we will find our old judgmental attitudes toward others gradually dropping away. Because we can accept ourselves as we are, we can accept others as they are, even though we may not like or approve of their actions. We understand that they are living their lives as they think best and that we can't reform them. Neither do we allow what we perceive as their wrong decisions to get to us. Instead, we willingly provide information about the program and our recovery, then give the work of convincing others that this is the proper path for them over to our Higher Power.

Societal Abuse

Once we've come to an awareness of emotional abuse and know deep in our hearts just how severe the problem is, once we understand from experience that it isn't "normal" and that we don't have to live with it, we often begin to understand how it pervades every aspect of our lives — not only our love relationships.

We see supervisors at work cutting down employees and disregarding their feelings, undermining their emotional well-being in addition to their productivity. We notice teachers who discount and minimize students in an attempt to control their thoughts as well as their classroom behavior. If only authority figures would develop and use more humane management skills . . .

We may begin to chafe under a societal system of beliefs which fosters emotionally abusing behavior in men and which reinforces the victim stance of women and children as the natural order of things. When we read the paper or listen to the news, we begin to pay attention to reports of domestic violence and sexual assault. As we heal, our tolerance for such behaviors as an inevitable part of life on this planet diminishes. We begin to wonder if there is a way to set things right.

We may grow angry at religions which discount women, labeling us the cause of original sin and denying us leadership roles. Suddenly blaming women for the downfall of humanity appears to us to be a mirror of the same blame game acted out in our own emotionally abusive relationships. We start to wonder if some religious leaders might not share many of the psychological characteristics as our abusing mates and we ache to do something about it.

In the broader context of society, we become sensitive to how some community leaders may distort the truth in order to push their agendas and, again, we are reminded of the destructive power games in our own households. We start to see how one ethnic or political group psychologically and verbally abuses another and wonder if there isn't some connection between the dynamics operating in those oppressor/oppressed situations and the one that operated in our love relationships. We begin to want to mend the angry rifts between people, to teach them to live in harmony.

National leaders engage in nasty verbal battles which erupt into violent physical confrontations between countries as each strives to dominate and control, to show the other who's boss. Watching the evening news, we can easily draw parallels between the troubled hotspots of the world and the way we lived before our recovery. The urge grows stronger inside of us to heal the world.

Everywhere we look, we see examples of individual people, groups and nations failing to coexist peacefully, refusing to respect each other's dignity and unaware of the common bonds we all share, our humanity and our Higher Power. Once we've traveled the Twelve Steps, we know that if others would only heed the message, they, too, could give up their need to control and that the ensuing cooperation would make our workplaces, schools, churches, neighborhoods and the world better places to be. Working the Twelve Steps has taught us that we do not need to be addicted to the role of victim or victimizer. There is a more rewarding and productive way to live.

Seeking Balance In Social Activism

Sometimes we are so distraught by events around us, we're tempted to stand up on a soapbox and devote our lives to fixing the world, just as we were tempted to try to repair our emotionally abusing partners. We forget that while at times public action is necessary, sometimes the more vehemently we talk about our philosophy and our faith, the less we may actually live by them. Early in our recovery, we need to guard against espousing causes so abstract that we start to live on the outside, rather than attending to the very necessary and concrete work we must continue to do on ourselves. Finding our individual balance between outreach and the inner life is essential if we are to progress in our recovery and to have a positive effect on those around us. Only when we're centered and grounded can we be truly effective in spreading the message.

Even when we must retreat and concentrate on getting our own recovery back on track, we are still making a positive contribution. From working the Twelve Steps we've learned to stop playing the victim game. The psychological abusers in our intimate relationships and in the broader world can no longer emotionally kick us around. When we live our lives as a strong and clear beacon, when we attract others toward our new way of operating in the world and we model it for them, we decrease the pool of victims that emotional abusers have to draw on. By simply being our recovering selves, we serve as an inspiration to others.

The very fact of our recovery is an elemental and positive move toward major social change. We may not be able to transform the world by making broad and sweeping reformations, but we have changed our lives and impacted on the lives of all those with whom we come in contact, minute by minute, day by day, one step at a time. Rather than dwelling on our frustration with the inequities of the world and beating ourselves up for not being able to heal it, we need to focus on the miraculous healing transformation of our own personal recovery and use that as a stepping stone. If our recovery isn't solid, we'll lose our balance when we try to carry the message to others.

The underpinnings of the Twelve-Step philosophy must serve as a basis for all of our decisions and actions about how to carry the message to those we encounter. When we are confused about where to begin, we need to ask our Higher Power for the answer and heed it when it comes. Not every woman's direction will be the same because each of us is blessed with different gifts. We need to be ever mindful that even though our contributions aren't identical with those of others in recovery, they are equally as precious.

The most logical place to start our outreach is by insuring that our family units are vital and healthy. Our example of how to live and to love serves as a powerful model for our children, future generations. When we decide to break the victimizer/victim cycle in our families, we influence many more people than we can imagine. Our children, our children's children, children yet unborn, will have a much greater chance of being raised in a functional family environment because we took the necessary steps to recover.

Twelve-Step Support Group

Many of us discover Twelve-Step Groups as an excellent means for spreading the recovery message as well as for healing ourselves. Through involvement with groups like Sex Addicts Anonymous and Co-dependents Anonymous, we can remain firm in our own recovery while reaching out to help others by serving as examples of how the program works. Whether we choose to make coffee, chair meetings, speak or eventually become a sponsor, the Twelve-Step work we do facilitates and enhances our own growth as well as that of other group members. With each effort we make, our self-esteem and sense of worth grows healthier. The more time and energy we give to our support groups, the better able we are to recognize the gifts with which we've been blessed.

Again, it is critical for us to keep helping others and fixing them straight in our minds. When we share our own experiences and talk about the solutions we've found,

we help others. When we give advice or *th*
attemping to fix them and are falling *into*
dependent patterns of manipulation and *cont*
reason, when we are in self-help groups, we *a*
to feel their pain and refrain from hugging *the*
they request to be touched. Our commitment *to*
help support group also needs to include not *com*
or making judgmental statements about what *other*
said, and we need to practice anonymity, keeping *the*
tities and issues of our fellow Twelve Steppers *confide*

Community Organization

Sometimes Twelve-Step work takes the form of *star*
ing a group where none exists, rather than sitting *aroun*
bemoaning the fact that there are no resources *available*
to us. Much of the power of these groups comes from *the*
fact that they aren't started by professionals or by people
who consider themselves to be completely healed. Instead
they are formed by individuals who see a need and who
feel called to fill it by contacting a parent organization for
informational support, then setting up a time and place
for a meeting and spreading the word.

Some of us may be called by our Higher Power to move
beyond our involvement in self-help groups and carry out
our Twelfth Step by actively participating as concerned
individuals in the workings of our community, our
churches, our schools and our nation. As with every
action we've taken since we began the Twelve-Step program, it is important for us to consult with our Higher
Power about just what we're intended to do and how
we're supposed to go about it.

For some women the call may come to serve on school
or church boards. We may create opportunities for ourselves to take a more meaningful part in the decision-
making processes which go on in our community. Some
of us become involved volunteering time to staff rape
crisis centers or battered women's centers. Others speak
and write letters to the editor about the problems of
emotional abuse, striving through education and social

legislation to balance the inequities at the root of the problem. The possibilities for involvement are endless.

Because we've developed a new way of looking at ourselves and at the world around us, we can develop a new way of healing the world, putting the principles contained in the Twelve Steps into practice in *all* of our affairs. Whether we're having problems at our place of employment, with a too-talkative member at our support group or a bitter struggle on a committee, we can work through it by going back to the Twelve Step basics and practicing them just as conscientiously as we did in our psychologically abusive relationships.

The Steps teach us that when we're caught up in power struggles and overly concerned about who is right and who is wrong, we become so busy blaming, we can't begin to solve our problems. When we live by the Steps, we are no longer powerless victims at the hands of the powerful. By admitting that we're powerless to change, manipulate and control others and by asking our Higher Power to restore sanity to our lives, we become empowered to act on the answers to our problems our Higher Power provides.

We're able, as well, to inventory ourselves and determine whether or not we're part of the problem we face. Rather than being bitter struggles, our lives become joyous and creative opportunities for growth from the smallest and most mundane daily details to the broadest issues we face as members of the human community.

The Twelve-Step Queries

Opportunities to practice the Twelve-Step principles present themselves on a daily basis. Often we can't change our external environments, but we can change our attitudes and actions. For that reason, it is important for us to make an effort to be always mindful of both the situations which confront us and the steps we can take to meet them.

Step One
We admitted we were powerless over _____ — that our lives had become unmanageable.

Are we being honest about our problems or are we burying our heads in the sand and denying them? Are we aware of the impact a particular problem may be having on other areas of our lives? Can we admit we have no power over others, or are we still trying to manipulate and control?

Step Two
We came to believe that a power greater than ourselves could restore us to sanity.

Can we honestly admit when we're using crazy thinking in an attempt to solve our problems? Do we have faith that the problem can be solved and that our Higher Power has the ability to solve it? Are we wise enough to look outside of ourselves for help?

Step Three
We made a decision to turn our will and our lives over to the care of God as we understood God.

Are we being stubborn and willful? Do we honestly believe that our Higher Power wants to care for us? Are we making a constant effort to know our Higher Power? Can we allow ourselves to let go and let God?

Step Four
We made a searching and fearless moral inventory of ourselves.

How are we contributing to the problem at hand? Are our thoughts, feelings and actions getting in the way of a solution? Is it possible that we've had a part in creating the problem?

Step Five
We admitted to God, to ourselves and to another human being the exact nature of our wrongs.

Can we honestly own our shortcomings in this matter? Are we willing to openly admit them? Do we allow ourselves to be honest with our Higher Power and to reach out to another person to hear our confession?

Step Six
We were entirely ready to have God remove all these defects of character.

Are we willing to let go of our defenses? Do we really want to stop our dysfunctional behavior or are we using it in order to manipulate and control others? Are we ready to act honestly and openly with those with whom we're having conflicts?

Step Seven
We humbly asked him to remove our shortcomings.

Will we allow our Higher Power to remove our short-comings or will we fight the process? Are we asking our Higher Power to change us for ourselves or are we desiring change only so that we can win the approval of others?

Step Eight
We made a list of all persons we had harmed and became willing to make amends to them all.

Can we accept our own failings and forgive ourselves? Are we willing to accept others and stop blaming them? Are we serious about mending our ways?

Step Nine
We made direct amends to such people wherever possible, except when to do so would injure them or others.

Do we take the risk of admitting our wrongs to those we've harmed? Do we make our admission without expectations of forgiveness or understanding? Are we ready to let go of our guilt?

Step Ten
We continued to take personal inventory and when we were wrong, promptly admitted it.

Do we acknowledge that most problems need long-term work and that we can and do make mistakes in the process? Have we given up our defense of always needing to be right? Do we quickly own up to our shortcomings or do we let our guilt fester into shame?

Step Eleven

We sought through prayer and meditation to improve our conscious contact with God as we understood God, praying only for knowledge of God's will for us and the power to carry that out.

Can we allow our relationship with our Higher Power to serve as the basis for our thoughts and the actions we take to solve our problems? Do we make a conscientious effort to set aside time to pray and meditate? Are we prepared to act on the solutions our Higher Power provides or are we too invested in our own to follow our Higher Power's?

Step Twelve

Having had a spiritual awakening as a result of these steps, we tried to carry this message to others, and to practice these principles in all our affairs.

Are we willing to allow our lives to serve as the message we carry when others refuse to listen to our words? Can we exercise tolerance for others or do we wish to reform them with missionary zeal? Do we put our spiritual awakening into action by using the Twelve Steps as a touchstone for all we do?

Bibliography

Beattie, Melody; **Beyond Co-dependency And Getting Better All The Time.** San Francisco: Harper/Hazelden, 1989.

Beattie, Melody; **Co-dependent No More.** San Francisco: Harper/Hazelden, 1987.

Bradshaw, John; **Healing The Shame That Binds You.** Deerfield Beach: Health Communications, 1988.

Castine, Jacqueline; **Recovery From Rescuing.** Deerfield Beach: Health Communications, 1989.

Covington, Stephanie and Beckett, Liana; **Leaving The Enchanted Forest.** New York: Harper & Row, 1988.

Covitz, Joel; **The Family Curse: Emotional Child Abuse.** Boston: Sigo Press, 1986.

Cowan, Connell, and Kinder, Melvyn; **Smart Women, Foolish Choices: Finding The Right Men And Avoiding The Wrong Ones.** New York: Signet, 1985.

Davidson, Joy; **The Agony Of It All: The Drive For Drama And Excitement In Women's Lives.** Los Angeles: Tarcher, 1988.

Dowling, Colette; **The Cinderella Complex: Women's Hidden Fear Of Independence.** New York: Pocket Books, 1981.

Fezler, William and Field, Eleanor; **The Good Girl Syndrome.** New York: Berkeley, 1985.

Fossum, Merle A., and Mason, Marilyn; **Facing Shame: Healing Families In Recovery.** New York: Norton, 1986.

Forward, Susan; **Men Who Hate Women And The Women Who Love Them.** New York: Bantam Books, 1985

Fortune, Marie; **Keeping The Faith.** New York: Harper & Row, 1987.

Friday, Nancy; **Jealousy.** New York: Bantam Books, 1985.

Goldstine, Daniel; Larne, Katherine; Zuckerman, Shirley and Goldstine, Hillary; **The Dance Away Lover And Other Roles We Play In Love, Sex And Marriage.** New York: Ballantine Books, 1977.

Hayes, Jody and Redl, Maureen; **Smart Love: Changing Painful Patterns, Choosing Healthy Relationships.** Los Angeles: Tarcher, 1989.

Hoffman, Susanna; **Men Who Are Good For You And Men Who Are Bad: Learning To Tell The Difference.** San Francisco: 10 Speed Press, 1987.

Kiley, Dan; **The Wendy Dilemma.** New York: Avon, 1984.

Kiley, Dan; **What To Do When He Won't Change.** New York: Fawcett, 1987.

Kolbenschlag, Madonna; **Kiss Sleeping Beauty Goodbye.** New York: Harper & Row, 1979.

Leman, Kevin; **The Pleasers: Women Who Can't Say No And The Men Who Control Them.** New York: Dell, 1987.

Leonard, Linda Schierse; **The Wounded Woman: Healing The Father Daughter Relationship.** Boston: Shambahla, 1985.

Lerner, Harriet; **The Dance Of Anger: A Woman's Guide To Changing Patterns Of Intimate Relationships.** New York: Harper & Row, 1985.

Miller, Joy; **Addictive Relationships: Reclaiming Your Boundaries.** Deerfield Beach: Health Communications, 1989.

NiCarthy, Ginny; **Getting Free: A Handbook For Women In Abusive Relationships.** Seattle: Seal Press, 1986.

NiCarthy, Ginny; **The Ones Who Got Away: Women Who Left Abusive Relationships.** Seattle: Seal Press, 1987.

Norwood, Robin; **Robin Norwood Answers Letters From Women Who Love Too Much.** New York: Pocket Books, 1988.

Norwood, Robin; **Women Who Love Too Much.** New York: Pocket Books, 1986.

O'Gorman, Patricia and Philip Oliver-Diaz; **12 Steps To Self-Parenting For Adult Children.** Deerfield Beach: Health Communications, 1988.

Peabody, Susan; **Addiction To Love.** San Francisco: 10 Speed Press, 1989.

Peele, Stanton: **Love And Addiction.** New York: New American Library, 1975.

Russianoff, Penelope; **Why Do I Think I Am Nothing Without A Man?** New York: Bantam Books, 1982.

Sanford, Linda Tschirhart and Donovan, Mary Ellen; **Women And Self Esteem: Improving The Way We Think And Feel About Ourselves.** New York: Penguin Books, 1986.

Schaef, Anne Wilson; **Co-dependence: Mistreated, Misunderstood.** San Francisco: Harper & Row, 1986.

Schaeffer, Brenda; **Is It Love Or Is It Addiction?** San Francisco: Harper & Row, 1987.

Schneider, Jennifer; **Back From Betrayal: Recovering From His Affairs.** San Francisco: Harper & Row, 1988.

Shaness, Natalie; **Sweet Suffering: Woman As Victim.** New York: Pocket Books, 1984.

Sonkin, Daniel J., Martin, Del and Walker, Lenore; **The Male Batterer.** New York: Springer, 1985.

Stuart, Mary; **In Sickness And In Health: The Co-dependent Marriage.** Deerfield Beach: Health Communications, 1988.

The Twelve Steps, A Way Out. San Diego: Recovery Publications, 1987.

Thoele, Sue Patton; **The Courage To Be Yourself.** Nevada City, CA: Pyramid Press, 1988.

Wegscheider-Cruse, Sharon; **Coupleship: How To Build A Relationship.** Pompano Beach: Health Communications, 1986.

Woititz, Janet Geringer; **Healing Your Sexual Self.** Deerfield Beach: Health Communications, 1989.

Woititz, Janet Geringer; **Struggle For Intimacy.** Pompano Beach: Health Communications, 1985.

Other Books by
Kay Marie Porterfield

**Keeping Promises: The Challenge
of a Sober Parent**

Coping With an Alcoholic Parent